MW01225615

Didax

SKILLS

S E R I E S

EDITING

GRADES 5-6

Published with the permission of R.I.C. Publications Pty. Ltd.

Copyright © 2007 by Didax, Inc., Rowley, MA 01969. All rights reserved.

First published by R.I.C. Publications Pty. Ltd., Perth, Western Australia. Revised by Didax Educational Resources.

Limited reproduction permission: The publisher grants permission to individual teachers who have purchased this book to reproduce the blackline masters as needed for use with their own students. Reproduction for an entire school or school district or for commercial use is prohibited.

Printed in the United States of America.

Order Number: 2-5281
ISBN-13: 978-1-58324-263-6

A B C D E F 11 10 09 08 07

395 Main Street
Rowley, MA 01969
www.didax.com

Foreword

Editing consists of a selection of texts written in specific formats to provide punctuation, spelling and grammatical practice. Detailed descriptions of concepts, such as specific parts of speech and punctuation, are also included, as well as vocabulary enrichment and aspects of writing.

The aim is to provide students with varied, structured experiences in proofreading and editing written texts. A high level of proficiency in these skills is vital for accurate self-monitoring of written work.

Other titles in this series are:

- *Editing, Grades 2 to 3*
- *Editing, Grades 3 to 4*
- *Editing, Grades 7 to 8*

Contents

Teacher Information

The following is an explanation of how to use the pages in this book.

Teacher Pages

A teacher page accompanies each student worksheet. It provides the following information:

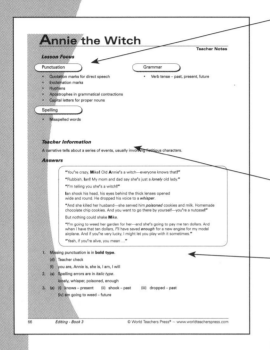

The Lesson Focus indicates the focus for each student page. This will include aspects from the areas of punctuation, spelling, grammar, vocabulary and writing. Some of these may involve simple recognition of a concept, or use an already-known aspect. More detailed teacher information about punctuation, spelling and grammar can be found on pages 8–11.

Teacher Information gives brief background information about each text type. More detailed information can be found on pages 12– 13.

Answers to all worksheet activities are provided. The corrected text is given with punctuation errors in bold. Correct spelling is highlighted in italics, as well as being provided in the answers section.

Proofreading and Editing Marks

Editors use a number of consistent symbols to indicate where changes are to be made in a text.

Teachers may require students to use these "professional" proofreading and editing marks to indicate errors in the text on the student pages.

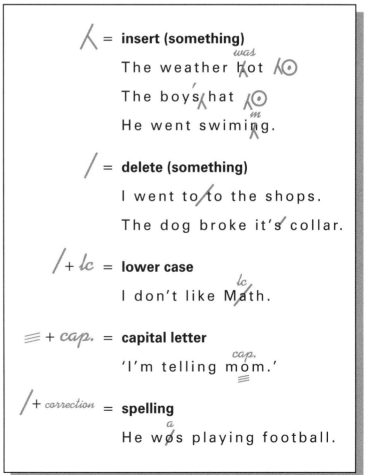

Teacher Information

Student Pages

- A specific text type is identified and presented for the students to read. The text has punctuation, spelling and grammatical errors for the student to identify.

  There are also opportunities presented for the students to work in the areas of grammar, vocabulary and writing as specified by the worksheet or teacher.

- The texts are presented in two ways. One allows students to become familiar with formats they may encounter in some standardized tests; both follow a similar format for identifying and correcting proofreading and editing errors.

The student activities follow a common format.

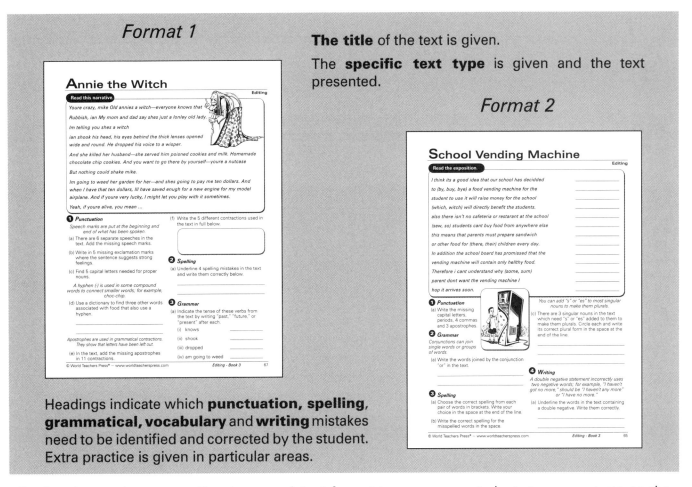

Format 1

The title of the text is given.

The **specific text type** is given and the text presented.

Format 2

Headings indicate which **punctuation, spelling, grammatical, vocabulary** and **writing** mistakes need to be identified and corrected by the student. Extra practice is given in particular areas.

Student instructions are written in a consistent format to encourage students to concentrate on the activity.

Where an instruction requires students to "**find** capital letters, etc.," teachers should select their own method for students to use; for example, circle, highlight with a colored marker, underline or write over the error. Some proofreading and editing marks may be used. (See Teacher Notes page 4.)

Activity Content Overview

Activity Content		23	25	27	29	31	33	35	37	39	41	43	45	47	49	51	53	55	57	59	61	63	65	67	69	71	73	75	77	79	81	83	85	87	89	91	93	95	97	99	101	103	105
PUNCTUATION																																											
Periods		●	●					●			●		●		●			●	●		●	●	●			●	●	●	●	●			●	●	●	●	●	●		●	●	●	●
Capital letters:	begin. of sentences	●	●	●	●		●	●				●			●	●			●		●	●	●			●	●		●	●			●	●	●	●	●	●		●		●	●
	proper nouns	●	●		●	●	●	●			●	●									●			●		●													●		●		
	in titles						●																																				
Question marks												●		●																	●						●						●
Exclamation marks												●													●	●											●						
Commas:	in a list	●	●		●		●	●					●		●			●					●		●		●		●				●		●								●
	grammatical	●						●			●		●					●			●		●		●		●			●			●		●			●		●			●
Apostrophes:	contractions		●		●	●		●	●	●	●			●	●			●				●	●	●		●	●			●	●										●		
	possession						●	●										●	●		●	●									●	●			●								
Quotation marks		●			●												●							●						●	●				●		●						
Colons:	in titles			●	●					●					●					●								●													●		●
	offset lists									●					●													●											●				
Brackets																											●	●															
Hyphens					●					●		●				●			●							●		●				●			●		●						
SPELLING																																											
Misspelled words		●	●	●	●	●	●	●	●	●	●	●	●	●	●	●	●	●	●	●	●	●	●	●	●	●	●	●	●	●	●	●	●	●	●	●	●	●	●	●		●	●
Confused words			●		●	●	●	●	●	●	●	●	●	●	●			●	●		●		●		●									●		●				●		●	●
Plurals:	adding "s" and "es"									●					●										●				●	●											●		
	change "y" to "i"														●																												
	"i" before "e"															●																											
TEXT TYPE		D	N	Expo.	Rep.	Rec.	Expl.	D	N	P	Rec.	D	N	Rep.	Expo.	N	Rec.	Expo.	Rep.	Rec.	D	N	Expo.	N	Rec.	D	Expl.	Rec.	Expl.	N	Expo.	Rep.	Expl.	P	Expl.	Rec.	N	Rep.	D	Expo.	P	Rep.	P

Page Number

Activity Content	105	103	101	99	97	95	93	91	89	87	85	83	81	79	77	75	73	71	69	67	65	63	61	59	57	55	53	51	49	47	45	43	41	39	37	35	33	31	29	27	25	23
GRAMMAR																																										
Nouns: common nouns	●					●	●																																			●
collective nouns																																				●						
Pronouns						●							●														●						●				●	●				●
Adjectives	●				●	●			●	●														●				●	●							●					●	
Verbs	●						●																																			
Verb tenses		●		●								●					●			●						●	●								●			●			●	
Subject-verb agreement				●					●				●		●	●		●												●				●					●	●		
Adverbs							●	●		●				●			●	●	●					●								●	●									
Prepositions									●						●			●				●	●										●									
Conjunctions		●							●			●									●	●			●	●									●							
Indefinite article: "a" or "an"			●																			●																				
VOCABULARY																																										
Enrichment	●			●				●															●							●			●									●
Synonyms									●																	●			●													
Antonyms																	●																									
Compound words																															●	●					●				●	
Shortened forms					●					●						●																										
WRITING																																										
Paragraphs											●																															
Double negatives			●		●																●						●								●		●			●		
TEXT TYPE	P	Rep	P	Expo	D	Rep	N	Rec	Expl	P	Expl	Rep	Expo	N	Expl	Rec	Expl	D	Rec	N	Expo	N	D	Rec	Rep	Expo	Rec	N	Expo	Rep	N	D	Rec	P	N	D	Expl	Rec	Rep	Expo	N	D

Narrative – N   Explanation – Expl.   Procedure – P   Recount – Rec.   Report – Rep.   Exposition – Expo.   Description – D

Teacher Information

Punctuation, Spelling and Grammar Information

PUNCTUATION

Please note: In some cases, teachers will need to exercise their own judgment with regard to punctuation, as certain aspects, particularly commas and exclamation marks, are to an extent discretionary and depend on the individual writer's intent.

Capital Letters

Capital letters are needed for:

- *sentence beginnings*; e.g., My dog is very friendly. He welcomes everyone.
- *proper nouns* – people's names (Chloe Parker), names of places (Indian Ocean), days of the week (Saturday), months (December), holidays and festivals (Christmas), countries (America), nationalities (Russian), languages (Italian) and religions (Buddhism).
- *titles*; e.g., World Health Organization

Commas

Commas are used to separate items in a list or series.

> I enjoy reading, playing squash, skiing and swimming.

Grammatical commas are used to:

- make the meaning of a sentence clear.

> Jane said her mother is very busy.   (Jane's mother is very busy.)
>
> Jane, said her mother, is very busy.   (Jane is very busy.)

- indicate where a pause is needed in a sentence.

> Many years ago, dinosaurs roamed the Earth.

Apostrophes for Possession

Apostrophes are used to show that something belongs to someone or something.

The placement of the apostrophe can be challenging but the simple rule is that it is placed after the owner or owners. (The "tail" of the apostrophe "points" to the owner[s].)

> the boy's shoes (one boy) .... the boys' shoes (more than one boy)
>
> the lady's hats   (one lady) .... the ladies' hats (more than one lady)

Grammatical Contractions

Grammatical contractions are words that have been made by joining and shortening two words. An apostrophe is used in place of the missing letters.

> would not.............wouldn't   will not ....won't
>
> I would ....I'd   they are................ they're

Exclamation Marks

Exclamation marks are used to end exclamations and imperatives (commands) and for emphasis at the end of a statement.

> I love it!
>
> Don't touch!
>
> She ate every bit of it!

Note: If overused, exclamation marks lose their effect.

Teacher Information

Quotation Marks

Quotation marks are used:
- to enclose quoted speech
- to enclose quotes within quotes, a double set is used outside and a single set inside.
    He reported, "My mother complained, 'Late again, John.'"

Colons

A *colon* is a marker of relationship and sequence. *Colons* are used:
- before offset lists
    You need to take:
    warm socks,
    sturdy walking shoes,
    a raincoat.
- between a statement and explanation
    I remember you: we went to the same school.
- with quotations
    Malcolm Fraser said: "Life wasn't meant to be easy."

Parentheses (round brackets)

The main use of *parentheses* is to enclose explanations and asides.
Parentheses are used to:
- add explanatory words
    Ian Thorpe (Australia) is a champion swimmer.
- express the same thing in a different way
    He ran 3 mi (miles).
- set off an aside
    He won the race in record (yet to be confirmed) time.

Hyphens

Hyphens are short strokes (without a space on either side) used to join words or parts of words.

    fun-loving   pre-existing

Note: Students should be encouraged to refer to a modern dictionary to check for current hyphenation, as it changes over time in response to common use.

Teacher Information

GRAMMAR

Nouns

Nouns are naming words of people, places and things; e.g., teacher, school, desk.

Proper nouns name individual people (Bill), places (Kings Park) and others (Christmas, December, Sunday). Proper nouns are written with capital letters.

Common nouns are any other nouns.

Collective nouns are a subset of common nouns; e.g., a *team* of players.

Pronouns

A *pronoun* is a word substituted for a noun; e.g., *They* asked *him* to help *them*.

Personal pronouns refer to you, me and other people; e.g., I, me, you, she, us, them.

Adjectives

Adjectives modify (enhance or change) the meaning of nouns and, less commonly, pronouns; e.g., *parched* land; *green*, *fertile* land; *poor old* me; *lucky* you.

Verbs

Verbs are "doing" words; e.g., swim, like, look.

Auxiliary verbs join other verbs to form verb groups; e.g., have eaten, will be asleep.

Verb tense. There are three basic tenses. Because there are so many irregular verbs in English, tense can be complex.

	the past..................... the present ....the future
regular	played ....play...............................will play has played ....plays........................ should play
irregular	went ....go...................................... will go has gone........................ goes...........................should go

NOTE: The future and the past tenses often use auxiliary verbs.

Subject-Verb Agreement

Verbs have to agree with their subjects

The children **cheer** loudly.   The child **cheers** loudly
   (subject-plural) verb   (subject-singular) verb

Many English verbs are irregular, which can cause problems, particularly for students from non-English speaking backgrounds.

He **is** at school.   They **are** at school.

He **was** busy.   They **were** busy.

In some sentences the subject of a verb is separated from the verb and not easy to locate. Students should be encouraged to ask themselves "who" or "what" before the verb.

The boy, although really late for school and likely to get into trouble, **dawdled**.

"dawdled" is the verb.

"The boy" is the subject. ("Who dawdled?")

Teacher Information

Adverbs

Adverbs are words that modify (enhance or change) the meaning of verbs.

He ran **quickly**.   I've seen this **before**.

There are adverbs of: time........................e.g., yesterday
                         place ....e.g., downstairs
                         manner.................e.g., carefully

Prepositions

Prepositions show the relationship between nouns and/or pronouns in the same sentence.

Common prepositions include: across, about, between, by, during, for, from, in, of, since, through, until, without, up.

He disappeared **during** the night.

I'm afraid **of** spiders.

I enjoy reading books **about** travel.

Conjunctions

Conjunctions are joining words. They can join different language units.

- One word with another ....e.g., black **or** white
- One phrase with another.......................e.g., on the beach **and** in the sand
- One clause with another ....e.g., He asked me **if** I could cook.
- One sentence with another...................e.g., I was hot **so** I went for a swim.

SPELLING

Singular and plural nouns

Adding "s" and "es"

The most commonly used plural is made by adding "s"; e.g., books, games.

It is usually necessary to add "es" to nouns ending in "ch," "sh," "s," "x" and "z" to make the plural easier to pronounce; e.g., washes, dishes, classes, foxes and waltzes.

Words ending in "o" are also often made into a plural by adding "es"; potatoes, tomatoes.

There are many exceptions, including radios, merinos, silos, zeros, photos and sopranos.

Students should be encouraged to consult a dictionary if uncertain about the spelling of a plural.

Changing "y" to "i" and adding "es"

Many nouns and verbs ending with "y," change the "y" to "i" before adding "es."

lady (singular noun).............................. ladies (plural noun)

curry (singular noun) .... curries (plural noun)

I cry .... he cries (verbs)

"i" before "e" except after "c"

Like most rules, there are many exceptions, but this rule is generally true.

perceive, thief, receive – seize, caffeine (exceptions)

Teacher Information

Writing Format Information

Below are general descriptions of the text types included in this book.

Narrative

- is a framework which tells a story.
- includes:
  - *Orientation*:
    the setting, time and character(s)
  - *Complication*:
    involving the main character(s) and a sequence of events.
  - *Resolution*:
    to the complication
  - *Ending*:
    often showing what has changed and what the characters have learned
- uses:
  - a range of conjunctions to connect ideas
  - appropriate paragraphing
  - descriptive language
  - past tense.

A narrative may be written in the form of a poem, story, play, imaginative story, fairy tale, novel, myth, legend, ballad, science fiction story, or modern fantasy.

Report

- is a framework which provides facts concerning aspects of a living or nonliving thing without unnecessary information or opinion.
- includes:
  - *Classification*:
    a general or classifying statement
  - *Description*:
    accurate and detailed
  - *Conclusion*:
    a comment about the content of the report (optional).
- uses:
  - factual language rather than imaginative
  - the third person
  - the timeless present tense
  - linking and action verbs.

A report may be written in the form of a book review, scientific report, newspaper or magazine article, eyewitness account, or a progress report.

Recount

- is a framework that retells events as they happened in time order.
- may be factual, personal or imaginative.
- includes:
  - *Orientation*:
    all relevant background (who, when, where, why)
  - *Events*:
    significant events in detail
  - *Conclusion*:
    often with an evaluative comment.
- uses:
  - vocabulary to suggest time passing
  - paragraphs to show separate sections
  - the past tense.

A recount may be written in the form of a newspaper report, diary, letter, journal, eyewitness account, biography, autobiography, or history.

Procedure

- is a framework which outlines how something is made or done.
- includes:
  - the purpose of the procedure shown clearly and precisely
  - a list of materials or requirements under appropriate headings or layout
  - the method in a detailed, logical sequence
  - an evaluation (if appropriate).
- uses:
  - instructions with an imperative verb
  - subject-specific vocabulary
  - simple present tense.

A procedure may be written in the form of a recipe, instructions for making something, an experiment, an instruction manual, a math procedure, how to play a game, how to operate an appliance, how to use an atlas and how to deal with a problem.

© World Teachers Press® ~ www.worldteacherspress.com

Teacher Information

Writing Format Information

Exposition

- is a framework which argues for a particular position and attempts to persuade the audience to share this view.
- includes:
  - *Introduction:*
    statement of the problem and the writer's position
  - *Arguments:*
    presented in a logical manner with supporting detail, usually from the strongest to the weakest
  - *Conclusion:*
    an evaluation restating the writer's position.
- uses:
  - persuasive language
  - paragraphs to state and elaborate on each point.

An exposition may be written in the form of an essay, a letter, a policy statement, a critical review, an advertisement, an editorial, or a speech.

Explanation

- is a framework which outlines how or why something occurs, works, or is made.
- includes:
  - *Statement:*
    precisely what is to be explained
  - *Explanation:*
    a clear account in logical sequence of how and why the phenomenon occurs
  - *Conclusion:*
    an evaluation and comment about what has been explained.

OR

- a definition
- a description of the components or parts
- the operation—how it works or is made
- the application—where and when it works or is applied
- special features—interesting comments
- evaluation or comment

- uses:
  - subject–specific terms and technical vocabulary where appropriate
  - simple present tense
  - linking words to show cause and effect.

An explanation may be written in the form of an essay, or a handbook (for example, how a kite works), a science text, a health text, or a social studies text.

Description

- is a framework which describes the characteristics, components or function of specific living or nonliving things.

Physical characteristics of living things are described; nonliving things are discussed in terms of their components and/or functions. Special features are also discussed. This type of writing can be used to describe, for example, a specific breed of animal, an object, or a picture.

- includes:
  - *Introduction:* what it is
  - *Description:* its appearance: color, shape, size, etc.
  - *Interesting details/special features*
  - *Concluding statement*.
- uses:
  - adjectives extensively
  - conjunctions.

A description may be written in poetic form and may describe a person, place, animal, thing, or emotion.

Student Narrative Checklist

Title: _____

Orientation:
The characters are introduced and described. ☐

Information about where the story happened is provided. ☐

The time the story took place is stated. ☐

Complication:
The complication involving the main characters is explained. ☐

Resolution:
The sequence of events is described. ☐

A logical, believable resolution is presented. ☐

Ending:
The narrative has a satisfactory ending. ☐

Writing skills:
• Paragraphs are used to introduce new ideas. ☐

• Descriptive language is included. ☐

• A range of conjunctions connects ideas. ☐

• The narrative is written in the past tense. ☐

• Adjectives are varied and interesting. ☐

• Punctuation and spelling have been checked. ☐

Name: _____ **Date:** _____

© World Teachers Press® ~ www.worldteacherspress.com

Student Narrative Checklist

Title: _____

Orientation:
The characters are introduced and described. ☐

Information about where the story happened is provided. ☐

The time the story took place is stated. ☐

Complication:
The complication involving the main characters is explained. ☐

Resolution:
The sequence of events is described. ☐

A logical, believable resolution is presented. ☐

Ending:
The narrative has a satisfactory ending. ☐

Writing skills:
• Paragraphs are used to introduce new ideas. ☐

• Descriptive language is included. ☐

• A range of conjunctions connects ideas. ☐

• The narrative is written in the past tense. ☐

• Adjectives are varied and interesting. ☐

• Punctuation and spelling have been checked. ☐

Name: _____ **Date:** _____

14   *Editing - Book 3*   © World Teachers Press® ~ www.worldteacherspress.com

Writing Format Checklists

Student Recount Checklist

Title:

☐ The title is suitable.

Orientation:

☐ A clearly written orientation provides relevant information about who, when, where and why.

Events:

☐ ☐ Significant events are described in detail.

Events are retold in chronological order.

Conclusion:

☐ ☐ The ending is clearly described.

An evaluative comment about the conclusion is included.

Writing skills:

☐ ☐ ☐ ☐ ☐ ☐
- Paragraphs are used to show separate sections.
- Vocabulary suggests the passing of time.
- The past tense is maintained.
- Sentence beginnings vary.
- Quotation marks are used for quoted speech.
- Punctuation and spelling have been checked.

Name: _____ **Date:** _____

Student Recount Checklist

Title:

☐ The title is suitable.

Orientation:

☐ A clearly written orientation provides relevant information about who, when, where and why.

Events:

☐ ☐ Significant events are described in detail.

Events are retold in chronological order.

Conclusion:

☐ ☐ The ending is clearly described.

An evaluative comment about the conclusion is included.

Writing skills:

☐ ☐ ☐ ☐ ☐ ☐
- Paragraphs are used to show separate sections.
- Vocabulary suggests the passing of time.
- The past tense is maintained.
- Sentence beginnings vary.
- Quotation marks are used for quoted speech.
- Punctuation and spelling have been checked.

Name: _____ **Date:** _____

Student Exposition Checklist

Title: _____

Overview:

The opening statement presents the topic and what I think about it. ☐

Arguments:

Arguments are presented in a logical manner. ☐

Supporting information is provided. ☐

The strongest arguments are presented first. ☐

Opposing arguments are rebutted. ☐

The language is persuasive. ☐

Conclusion:

A summary of the supporting arguments is given. ☐

A evaluative conclusion is presented. ☐

Writing skills:

- Paragraphs state and elaborate each point. ☐
- The writing style is impersonal. ☐
- A variety of conjunctions is used. ☐
- Punctuation and spelling have been checked. ☐

Name: _____ **Date:** _____

Student Exposition Checklist

Title: _____

Overview:

The opening statement presents the topic and what I think about it. ☐

Arguments:

Arguments are presented in a logical manner. ☐

Supporting information is provided. ☐

The strongest arguments are presented first. ☐

Opposing arguments are rebutted. ☐

The language is persuasive. ☐

Conclusion:

A summary of the supporting arguments is given. ☐

A evaluative conclusion is presented. ☐

Writing skills:

- Paragraphs state and elaborate each point. ☐
- The writing style is impersonal. ☐
- A variety of conjunctions is used. ☐
- Punctuation and spelling have been checked. ☐

Name: _____ **Date:** _____

16   *Editing - Book 3*   © World Teachers Press® ~ www.worldteacherspress.com

Student Explanation Checklist

☐ ☐ ☐ ☐ ☐ ☐ ☐ ☐ ☐ ☐

Title: _____

Definition:

A precise statement or definition is provided.

Description:

There is a clear account of how and why the phenomenon occurs.

Information is relevant and correct.

Information is provided in a logical order.

Explanations are clearly and simply stated.

Concluding statement:

The conclusion includes an evaluation or comment.

Writing skills:

• Linking words are used to show cause and effect.

• The simple present tense is used.

• Technical vocabulary and subject-specific terms are used.

• Spelling and punctuation have been checked.

Name: _____ **Date:** _____

Writing Format Checklists

Student Explanation Checklist

☐ ☐ ☐ ☐ ☐ ☐ ☐ ☐ ☐ ☐

Title: _____

Definition:

A precise statement or definition is provided.

Description:

There is a clear account of how and why the phenomenon occurs.

Information is relevant and correct.

Information is provided in a logical order.

Explanations are clearly and simply stated.

Concluding statement:

The conclusion includes an evaluation or comment.

Writing skills:

• Linking words are used to show cause and effect.

• The simple present tense is used.

• Technical vocabulary and subject-specific terms are used.

• Spelling and punctuation have been checked.

Name: _____ **Date:** _____

Student Report Checklist

Title: _____

Classification:

There is a general or classifying statement about the subject of the report. ☐

Description:

Provides accurate, detailed descriptions. ☐
Information is clearly presented. ☐
Facts are relevant and interesting. ☐

Conclusion:

A personal comment has been made about the subject. ☐

Writing skills:

- Language is factual rather than imaginative. ☐
- The report is written in the third person. ☐
- The present tense is used. ☐
- Technical vocabulary and subject-specific terms are used. ☐
- Information is organized in paragraphs. ☐
- Punctuation and spelling have been checked. ☐

Name: _____ **Date:** _____

Student Report Checklist

Title: _____

Classification:

There is a general or classifying statement about the subject of the report. ☐

Description:

Provides accurate, detailed descriptions. ☐
Information is clearly presented. ☐
Facts are relevant and interesting. ☐

Conclusion:

A personal comment has been made about the subject. ☐

Writing skills:

- Language is factual rather than imaginative. ☐
- The report is written in the third person. ☐
- The present tense is used. ☐
- Technical vocabulary and subject-specific terms are used. ☐
- Information is organized in paragraphs. ☐
- Punctuation and spelling have been checked. ☐

Name: _____ **Date:** _____

18 *Editing - Book 3* © World Teachers Press® ~ www.worldteacherspress.com

Student Procedure Checklist

Title: ☐

Goal:

☐ The purpose is clearly and precisely stated.

Materials:

☐ The materials or requirements are listed under appropriate headings or layout.

Method:

☐ The steps are clear and concise.

☐ There is a logical order to the sequence of the steps.

☐ The steps are easy to understand and follow.

☐ All of the necessary steps are included.

Test:

☐ An evaluation to test if the procedure has been successfully followed is included.

Writing skills:

☐ • Instructions begin with command verbs.

☐ • The present tense is used.

☐ • Unnecessary words have been omitted.

☐ • Punctuation and spelling have been checked.

Name: _____ **Date:** _____

Student Procedure Checklist

Title: ☐

Goal:

☐ The purpose is clearly and precisely stated.

Materials:

☐ The materials or requirements are listed under appropriate headings or layout.

Method:

☐ The steps are clear and concise.

☐ There is a logical order to the sequence of the steps.

☐ The steps are easy to understand and follow.

☐ All of the necessary steps are included.

Test:

☐ An evaluation to test if the procedure has been successfully followed is included.

Writing skills:

☐ • Instructions begin with command verbs.

☐ • The present tense is used.

☐ • Unnecessary words have been omitted.

☐ • Punctuation and spelling have been checked.

Name: _____ **Date:** _____

© World Teachers Press® ~ www.worldteacherspress.com — *Editing - Book 3* — 19

Student Description Checklist

Title: _____

Introduction:

The introduction states what is to be described.   ☐

Description:

Details concerning appearance are provided.   ☐

Interesting details are included.   ☐

Special features are described.   ☐

Writing skills:

- Information is interesting.   ☐
- Relevant details are provided.   ☐
- Adjectives are used extensively.   ☐
- Conjunctions link ideas.   ☐
- Appropriate paragraphing is used.   ☐
- Punctuation and spelling have been checked.   ☐

Name: _____ **Date:** _____

Student Description Checklist

Title: _____

Introduction:

The introduction states what is to be described.   ☐

Description:

Details concerning appearance are provided.   ☐

Interesting details are included.   ☐

Special features are described.   ☐

Writing skills:

- Information is interesting.   ☐
- Relevant details are provided.   ☐
- Adjectives are used extensively.   ☐
- Conjunctions link ideas.   ☐
- Appropriate paragraphing is used.   ☐
- Punctuation and spelling have been checked.   ☐

Name: _____ **Date:** _____

20   *Editing - Book 3*   © World Teachers Press® ~ www.worldteacherspress.com

Student Proofreading and Editing Checklist

Use this page to check your work. You will not need to check all of the boxes.

Name: _____ **Date:** _____

Title: _____

Punctuation:
I have included:
- capital letters for: beginning sentences.
                          proper nouns.
                          titles.
- question marks.
- periods.
- commas: in lists.
            for pauses.
            to make meaning clear.
- apostrophes: for grammatical contractions.
                 to show ownership.
- exclamation marks.
- quotation marks.
- colons: in titles.
            for off-set lists.
- parentheses.
- hyphens.

Spelling:
I have:
- checked the spelling of any unknown words.
- not confused words that sound the same.
- used correct endings for plurals

Grammar:
I have included:
- a variety of different verbs.
- correct verb tenses.
- correct verb-subject agreement.
- appropriate adverbs to describe verbs.
- suitable nouns.
- appropriate pronouns.
- interesting adjectives.
- suitable conjunctions.
- a variety of prepositions.

Writing:
I have read through my writing to check that:
- it makes sense.
- it is easy to understand.
- paragraphing is appropriate.
- there are no double negatives.

Tasmanian Devil

Lesson Focus

Punctuation

- Capital letters for proper nouns
- Capital letters for sentence beginnings
- Periods
- Grammatical commas
- Commas in lists
- Exclamation marks

Spelling

- Misspelled words

Grammar

- Pronouns

Vocabulary

- Enrichment – Australian animals

Teacher Information

A description describes the characteristics, components or functions of specific living or non-living things.

Answers

Tasmanian devils are nocturnal *marsupials* about the size of a small dog. <u>They</u> are found only in **T**asmania**.** **D**evils have black fur, *often* with white patches on their chest and rump. <u>They</u> have large heads and short**,** thick tails. Devils can make different *spinechilling noises***,** ranging from growls to screeches. Devils are carnivorous animals**.** **T**hey *generally* eat whatever meat they can find**,** including dead animals. <u>They</u> have been *known* to eat a range of reptiles**,** birds**,** *mammals* and insects**.** **A** devil will use its strong jaws and teeth to eat *almost* all the parts of an *animal*—even its bones and fur**!**

marsupials	
They	
often	
They	
spinechilling	
noises	
generally	
They	
known	
mammals	
almost	
animal	

1. Missing punctuation is in **bold type**.

2. (a) my class – we, Tasmanian devils – They, Joshua – he, Tasmanian devils – them

    (b) Pronouns are <u>underlined</u>.

    They (line 2), They (line 4), They (line 8)

    (c) Teacher check

3. Spelling errors are in *italic type*.

    marsupial, often, spine-chilling, noises, generally, known, mammals, almost, animal

4. (a) Teacher check

Tasmanian Devil

Read the description.

Tasmanian devils are nocturnal marsupals about _____

the size of a small dog. It are found only in tasmania _____

devils have black fur, offen with white patches on _____

their chest and rump. It have large heads and _____

short thick tails. Devils can make different spinechiling _____

noisis ranging from growls to screeches. Devils are _____

carnivorous animals they genrally eat whatever _____

meat they can find including dead animals. It _____

have been nown to eat a range of reptiles birds _____

mamals and insecs a devil will use its strong jaws _____

and teeth to eat allmost all the parts of an _____

annimal—even its bones and fur _____

① Punctuation

(a) Find the 4 missing capital letters, 3 periods, 5 commas and 1 exclamation mark.

② Grammar

Pronouns are words that replace nouns; for example, "I," "he," "she," "him," "it."

(a) Use a suitable pronoun to replace the bold words.

Last year **my class** learned about Tasmanian devils. **Tasmanian devils** look cute but Joshua said that **Joshua** wouldn't like to keep **Tasmanian devils** as pets.

(b) Circle the incorrect pronouns used in the text. Write the correct pronouns in the space at the end of the line.

(c) Use the information from the text to write your own sentence about Tasmanian devils using at least one pronoun.

_____

_____

_____

③ Spelling

(a) Underline the spelling mistake in each line of text and write the correction in the space at the end of the line.

④ Vocabulary

(a) Write a list of at least 8 native Australian animals.

_____

_____

_____

_____

Dream Catcher

Lesson Focus

Punctuation

- Capital letters for proper nouns
- Capital letters for sentence beginnings
- Periods
- Grammatical commas

Grammar

- Adjectives
- Verb tenses

Spelling

- Misspelled words
- Confused words: two/to, maid/made, wood/would, there/their, threw/through, too/to

Vocabulary

- Compound words
- Hyphenated words

Teacher Information

Narratives tell a story in a sequence of events often involving fictitious characters.

Answers

Long ago**,** Iktomi, the teacher of *wisdom***,** appeared *to* a <u>Lakota</u> elder. **I**ktomi had taken the form of a spider. The spider *took* a <u>wooden</u> hoop that the elder was carrying**.** **I**t then <u>started</u> to spin a web in it.	wisdom
	to
	took
	started
The spider *made* the web a <u>perfect</u> circle with a hole in the middle. It told the elder that webs like this *would* help the Lakota people <u>reach</u> their goals and make <u>better</u> use of *their* ideas and dreams. The webs would *catch* their <u>good</u> ideas and dreams and let the <u>bad</u> ones go straight *through* the hole. The elder <u>took</u> the web to his people and told them what the spider had *said*. **T**he **L**akota people then made their own "*dream* catchers."	made
	would
	reach
	their
	catch
	through
	took
	said
	dream
Today, many <u>native</u> **A**mericans hang dream catchers above their beds *to* capture good dreams and ideas.	Today
	to

1. Missing punctuation is in **bold type**.

2. (a) Adjectives are <u>underlined</u>.

    Answers should include three of the following: Lakota, wooden, perfect, better, good, bad, dream, native

   (b) Verbs are <u>underlined in bold</u>.

    will start – started (line 4); will reach – reach (line 7); will take – took (line 11)

3. (a) Spelling errors are in *italic type*.

    wisdom, to, took, made, would, their, catch, through, said, dream, Today, to

4. Answers will vary but may include dreamboat, Dreamtime, webfoot, website and web-toed.

Dream Catcher

Read the legend from North America.

Long ago Iktomi, the teacher of wisdem appeared _____

two a Lakota elder. iktomi had taken the form of a _____

spider. The spider tok a wooden hoop that the _____

elder was carrying it then will start to spin a web in it. _____

The spider maid the web a perfect circle with a hole _____

in the middle. It told the elder that webs like this wood _____

help the Lakota people will reach their goals and _____

make better use of there ideas and dreams. The webs _____

would cach their good ideas and dreams and let the _____

bad ones go straight threw the hole. The elder _____

will take the web to his people and told them what _____

the spider had sed the lakota people then made _____

their own "dreem catchers." _____

Tooday many native americans hang dream catchers _____

above their beds too capture good dreams and ideas. _____

❶ Punctuation

(a) Find the missing capital letters, periods and commas.

❷ Grammar

*Adjectives are words that describe nouns; for example, "**red** car," "**juicy** apple."*

(a) Circle 3 adjectives in the text.

*Verbs in the future tense describe what will happen in the future. The word "will" is often used to show this; for example, "He **will** go," "She **will** see."*

(b) Three of the verbs in the text have been written incorrectly in the future tense. Circle them and write the correct verb tense in the space at the end of the line.

❸ Spelling

(a) Write the misspelled words correctly in the space at the end of the lines.

❹ Vocabulary

(a) Write at least 3 more compound words, either hyphenated or unhyphenated, that begin with the words "dream" or "web." Use a dictionary.

dreamland,

Robotic Pets

Lesson Focus

Punctuation

- Grammatical commas
- Apostrophes to show possession
- Apostrophes in grammatical contractions
- Question marks
- Capital letters in titles
- Colons in titles

Spelling

- Misspelled words

Grammar

- Subject-verb agreement

Writing

- Double negatives

Teacher Information

An exposition evaluates an issue. Arguments are given to persuade the audience to a particular point of view.

Answers

> **R**obotic Pets**:** My Opinion
>
> Robotic pets, like cats and dogs**,** are now *available*. But
> I think they should be banned. If a robotic pet <u>is</u> bought
> for a *young* child**,** it could *teach* him or her that pets can be
> ignored or mistreated whenever the child**'**s mood changes. What would *happen* if one
> day the child <u>receives</u> a real pet**?** He or she may treat it the same way.
>
> Some robotic pets are used in nursing homes for *elderly* people who are unable to
> care for a real pet. I understand that this may give them some *comfort*, <u>but a robotic</u>
> <u>pet can't give you love</u> like a real animal can. I think nursing homes should <u>have</u>
> *volunteers* who regularly <u>bring</u> in real pets for a few hours at a time *instead*.
>
> The only *positive* thing about robotic pets is that it might save some animals from
> being treated *cruelly* by their owners. But the cost of robotic pets is still too high for
> most people**'**s *budgets*.

1. (a) Missing punctuation is in **bold type**.

2. (a) Verbs are <u>underlined</u>.

   are – is (line 2), receive – receives (line 5), has – have (line 8), brings – bring (line 9)

3. (a) Spelling errors are in *italic type*.

   available, young, teach, happen, elderly, comfort, volunteers, instead, positive, cruelly, budgets

4. (a) One way of correcting the double negative is <u>underlined in bold</u>.

   …"but a robotic pet can't give you no love …" should read "but a robotic pet can't give you love …"

   (b) Teacher check

   (i) They had no pets/They never had pets/They never had any pets

   (ii) He didn't see robots/He saw no robots/He didn't see any robots

Robotic Pets

Read the exposition.

robotic Pets My Opinion

Robotic pets, like cats and dogs are now availlable. But
I think they should be banned. If a robotic pet are bought
for a yung child it could teech him or her that pets can be
ignored or mistreated whenever the childs mood changes. What would hapen if one
day the child receive a real pet He or she may treat it the same way.

Some robotic pets are used in nursing homes for eldely people who are unable to
care for a real pet. I understand that this may give them some cumfort, but a robotic
pet cant give you no love like a real animal can. I think nursing homes should has
volunters who regularly brings in real pets for a few hours at a time insted.

The only positiv thing about robotic pets is that it might save some animals from
being treated cruely by their owners. But the cost of robotic pets is still too high for
most peoples budjets.

❶ Punctuation

(a) Write the 2 missing commas, 3 apostrophes and 1 question mark. Correct the title by writing the missing capital letter and colon.

❷ Grammar

In any sentence, the subject and the verb have to agree in person and in number; for example, "he sees" but "they see."

(a) Four verbs in the text do not agree with their subjects. Write the correct form of each.

❸ Spelling

(a) Write the correct spelling of the 11 misspelled words.

_____

_____

_____

_____

_____

❹ Writing

*A double negative statement incorrectly uses two negative words; for example, "I **haven't** got **no** more" should be "I haven't any more" or "I have no more."*

(a) Underline the line in the text containing a double negative. Write it correctly.

_____

(b) Correct the double negatives.

(i) They never had no pets.

_____

(ii) He didn't see no robots.

_____

Mars

Lesson Focus

Punctuation

- Capital letters for proper nouns
- Capital letters for sentence beginnings
- Periods
- Commas in lists
- Colons in titles
- Hyphens

Grammar

- Subject-verb agreement

Spelling

- Misspelled words

Writing

- Paragraphing

Teacher Information

A report gives facts clearly without unnecessary information or opinions.

Answers

Mars: the Red Planet

Mars is the fourth planet from the sun. **Y**ou can <u>see</u> Mars from **E**arth as a reddish-orange *color*. This is because it <u>has</u> red soil.

_____ see _____
_____ color _____
_____ has _____

Mars would not be a *pleasant* place to visit. **T**he air is mostly carbon dioxide, there are lots of *giant* dust storms and the average temperature <u>is</u> –60 °C.

_____ pleasant _____
_____ giant _____
_____ is _____

But **M**ars <u>has</u> a few things in common with **E**arth. It has *clouds*, canyons, valleys, plains, mountains, polar ice-caps and even volcanoes! Scientists <u>have</u> also found frozen water under the *surface* of the planet.

_____ has _____
_____ clouds _____
_____ have _____
_____ surface _____

1. (a) Missing punctuation is in bold type.

    (b) (i) reddish-orange, ice-caps

    (ii) Teacher check

2. (a) Verbs are <u>underlined</u>.

    sees – see (line 1), have – has (line 3), are – is (line 6), have – has (line 7), has – have (line 9)

3. (a) Spelling errors are in *italic type*.

    color, pleasant, giant, clouds, surface

4. (a) Answers will vary, but should indicate the following:

    paragraph 2 – "What would it be like to visit Mars?"

    paragraph 3 – "What does Mars have in common with Earth?"

Mars

Read the report.

Mars the red planet

Mars is the fourth planet from the sun you can sees
Mars from earth as a reddishorange culour. This is
because it have red soil.

mars would not be a plesant place to visit the air is
mostly carbon dioxide, there are lots of jiant dust
storms and the average temperature are –60 °C.

But mars have a few things in common with earth. It
has clowds canyons valleys plains mountains polar
icecaps and even volcanoes! Scientists has also
found frozen water under the surfase of the planet.

_____
_____
_____
_____
_____
_____
_____
_____
_____

❶ Punctuation

(a) Find the 8 missing capital letters, 5 commas and 2 periods. Put a colon in the correct place in the title.

A hyphen (-) is used in some words to connect smaller words; for example, "happy-go-lucky," "self-pity," "blue-black."

(b) (i) There are two words in this text that need a hyphen between them but they have been incorrectly written as one word. Add the hyphens.

(ii) Find three hyphenated words starting with "w" in a dictionary.

❷ Grammar

In any sentence, the subject and the verb have to agree in person and in number; for example, "He **sees**" but "They **see**."

(a) Five verbs in the text do not agree with their subjects. Write the correct form of each verb in the space at the end of the line.

❸ Spelling

(a) Write the misspelled words correctly in the space at the end of the line.

❹ Writing

(a) This text is divided into paragraphs. Each paragraph describes a new thought or idea. The first paragraph answers the question "Where and what is Mars?" Write a question that is answered by each of the last two paragraphs.

Paragraph 2 _____

_____

Paragraph 3 _____

_____

Crown Princess Mary of Denmark

Lesson Focus

Punctuation

- Capital letters for proper nouns
- Grammatical commas
- Commas in lists
- Apostrophes to show possession
- Quotation marks

Grammar

- Pronouns
- Verb tenses

Spelling

- Misspelled words

Teacher Information

A biography is a type of recount. A recount retells events as they happened in time order. Recounts are written using verbs in the past tense.

Answers

> Mary **D**onaldson was *born* in Hobart, Tasmania, on **F**ebruary 5, 1972. <u>She</u> completed her schooling in Tasmania, where she enjoyed *competing* in horse riding**,** swimming and *hockey*. On leaving *secondary* school, Mary <u>attended</u> the University of **T**asmania and graduated in 1994 with degrees in commerce and law. Soon after**,** she <u>moved</u> to **M**elbourne and worked for an international *advertising* agency. Mary then worked in *various* jobs in Australia and Europe.
>
> In 2000**,** Mary met Crown Prince **F**rederik of Denmark in a Sydney pub. She didn't know at first that he was a prince— <u>he</u> introduced himself as **"**Fred**"**! The couple <u>were</u> *married* in Copenhagen on May 14, 2004. Becoming the Crown Princess of **D**enmark meant huge changes to Mary**'**s life. <u>She</u> gave up her **A**ustralian citizenship**,** changed her *religion* and learned **D**anish.

1. (a) Missing punctuation and punctuation to identify is in **bold type**.

2. (a) Pronouns are <u>underlined</u>.

    It – She (line 1), him – he (line 9), Her – She (line 12)

    (b) (i) present tense   (ii) past tense

    (iii) future tense

    (c) Verbs are <u>underlined in bold</u>.

    will attend – attended (line 3), moves – moved (line 5), are – were (line 9)

3. (a) Spelling errors are in *italic type*.

    born, competing, hockey, secondary, advertising, various, married, religion

Crown Princess Mary of Denmark

Read the recount.

Mary donaldson was bourn in Hobart, Tasmania, on february 5, 1972. It completed her schooling in Tasmania, where she enjoyed competting in horse riding swimming and hocky. On leaving secondry school, Mary will attend the University of tasmania and graduated in 1994 with degrees in commerce and law. Soon after she moves to melbourne and worked for an international advertizing agency. Mary then worked in varius jobs in Australia and Europe.

In 2000 Mary met Crown Prince frederik of Denmark in a Sydney pub. She didn't know at first that he was a prince— him introduced himself as "Fred"! The couple are maried in Copenhagen on May 14, 2004. Becoming the Crown Princess of denmark meant huge changes to Marys life. Her gave up her australian citizenship changed her relijion and learned danish.

❶ Punctuation

(a) Find 8 missing capital letters, 4 commas and 1 apostrophe to show possession. Circle the quotation marks.

❷ Grammar

Pronouns are words that replace nouns; for example, "I," "he," "she," "him," "it."

(a) Circle the 3 incorrect pronouns used in the text.

*We can change the "tense" of a verb to tell what happened in the past, what is happening in the present or what will happen in the future; for example, "he **gave** her a gift" (past tense); "he **gives** her a gift" (present tense); "he **will give** her a gift" (future tense).*

(b) Write "past," "present," or "future" after each verb.

(i) looks _____

(ii) have done _____

(iii) will be _____

(c) All of the verbs in the text should be in the past tense, but there are 3 examples where the wrong verb tense has been used. Write each of the incorrect verbs from the text. Next to each, write the correct verb tense.

(i) _____ _____

(ii) _____ _____

(iii) _____ _____

❸ Spelling

(a) Write the correct spelling of the 8 misspelled words.

Why Do Stars Twinkle?

Lesson Focus

Punctuation

- Capital letters for proper nouns
- Capital letters for titles
- Grammatical commas
- Apostrophes to show possession

Grammar

- Pronouns

Spelling

- Confused words: threw/through, which/witch
- Misspelled words

Vocabulary

- Compound words

Writing

- Double negatives

Teacher Information

An explanation tells how and why something happens.

Answers

> **T**winkle, **T**winkle, **L**ittle **S**tar
>
> You may be *surprised* to learn that stars <u>actually never do any twinkling</u> at all! When you look at a star**,** <u>you</u> are seeing <u>it</u> through the thick layers of air that make up the **E**arth**'**s *atmosphere*. When the star**'**s light passes *through* these layers of air**,** the light is bent or "refracted" *differently* by each layer. This is because of *moisture* in the air as well as different air temperatures and the movement of the air. Together**,** <u>they</u> make the starlight seem to be moving, *which* we see as twinkling.
>
>   surprised
>   you
>   it
>   atmosphere
>   through
>   differently
>   moisture
>   they
>   which

1. Missing punctuation is in **bold type**.

2. (a) Pronouns are <u>underlined</u>.

    (i) you (line 2), it (line 3), they (line 8)

    (ii) Teacher check

3. Spelling errors are in *italic type*.

    (a) surprised, atmosphere, through, differently, moisture, which

4. (a) Teacher check

5. (a) One way of correcting the double negative is <u>**underlined in bold**</u>.

    "… stars actually never do no twinkling …" should read "… stars actually never do any twinkling …," or "… stars actually do no twinkling …"

Why Do Stars Twinkle?

Read the explanation.

twinkle, twinkle, little star

You may be suprised to learn that stars actually never _____

do no twinkling at all! When you look at a star they are _____

seeing them through the thick layers of air that make _____

up the earths atmosfere. When the stars light _____

passes threw these layers of air the light is bent or _____

"refracted" diffrently by each layer. This is because of _____

mosturre in the air as well as different air temperatures _____

and the movement of the air. Together it make the _____

starlight seem to be moving, witch we see as twinkling. _____

❶ Punctuation

(a) Find 4 missing capital letters in the title and 1 for a proper noun, 3 missing commas and 2 apostrophes to show possession.

❷ Grammar

Pronouns are words that replace nouns; for example, "I," "he," "she," "him," "it."

(a) (i) Circle the incorrect pronouns used in the text. Write the correct pronouns on the line at the end of each row.

　　(ii) Use the information from the text to write your own sentence about stars, using a pronoun.

_____

_____

_____

_____

❸ Spelling

(a) Write the correct spelling for the misspelled words in the space at the end of each line.

❹ Vocabulary

(a) Write as many compound words, either hyphenated or unhyphenated, as you can think of beginning with the word "star." You can use a dictionary.

> starlight, star-spangled,

❺ Writing

*A double negative statement incorrectly uses two negative words. For example, "I **haven't** got **no** more," should be "I haven't any more," or "I have no more."*

(a) Underline the line in the text containing a double negative. Write it correctly.

_____

_____

Windswept Poem

Lesson Focus

Punctuation

- Capital letters at the beginning of a line of poetry
- Apostrophes to show possession

Grammar

- Verb tenses
- Conjunctions

Spelling

- Misspelled words
- Confused words: hair/hare, me/my

Writing

- Double negatives

Teacher Information

This free verse poem is a narrative.

Answers

The Wind

The wind *swirls* around me	swirls
And *invites* me to play.	invites
Ruffles my *hair*	hair
<u>Tickles</u> my cheeks	Tickles
Tugs at *my* shirt	my
And *whispers* in my ear.	whispers
But I *don't* <u>do anything</u>	don't
And the wind**'**s temper *rises*.	rises
<u>Kicks</u> sand in my face	Kicks
Pushes at my chest	Pushes
Whips my arms	Whips
And howls with *laughter*	laughter
As I struggle to my feet and stamp down the *beach*.	beach

1. Missing punctuation is in **bold type**.

2. (a) Verbs are <u>underlined</u>.

   Tickled – Tickles, Kicked – Kicks, Whipped – Whips

   (b) The present tense verbs are swirls, invites, ruffles, tugs, whispers, do, rises, pushes, howls, struggle, stamp. Teachers will need to check the synonyms the students have chosen.

   (c) Answers include: and, but, as

   (d) Teacher check. Possible answer: I need to open the door **before/so** I can walk inside.

3. (a) Spelling mistakes are in *italic type*.

   swirls, invites, hair, my, whispers, don't, rises, pushes, laughter, beach

4. (a) One way of correcting the double negative is <u>**underlined in bold**</u>.

   "I don't <u>do anything</u>" or "I <u>do nothing</u>."

Windswept Poem

Read the poem.

The Wind

The wind swurls around me _____

And invittes me to play. _____

Ruffles my hare _____

Tickled my cheeks _____

tugs at me shirt _____

And whisppers in my ear. _____

But I do'nt do nothing _____

And the winds temper rizes. _____

Kicked sand in my face _____

pushs at my chest _____

whipped my arms _____

And howls with larfter _____

As I struggle to my feet and stamp down the beech. _____

❶ Punctuation
(a) Find the 3 missing capital letters and 1 apostrophe to show possession.

❷ Grammar
The verbs in this poem should all be written in the present tense; for example, "drinks," "sits."

(a) Underline 3 verbs in the poem that are not in the present tense. Write them in the present tense in the space at the end of the lines.

Synonyms are words with the same or similar meaning; for example, "yells," "bellows."

(b) Find three present tense verbs in the poem. Write a synonym for each.

_____ _____

_____ _____

_____ _____

(c) Write 2 conjunctions used in the text.

_____ _____

(d) Use a conjunction to join these 2 sentences.

> **I need to open the door.**
> **I can walk inside.**

_____

_____

❸ Spelling
(a) Underline the 10 misspelled words and write the correct spelling on the line provided.

❹ Writing
*A double negative statement incorrectly uses two negative words; for example, "I haven't got no more," should be "I **haven't** any more," or "I have **no** more."*

(a) Circle the line in the text containing a double negative. Write it correctly.

_____

_____

Guard the Treasure!

Lesson Focus

Punctuation

- Capital letters for sentence beginnings
- Grammatical commas
- Apostrophes to show possession
- Hyphens
- Colons for offset lists

Grammar

- Subject-verb agreement

Spelling

- Misspelled words
- Plurals ("s" and "es")

Teacher Information

A procedure outlines how something is done. It gives a list of materials or requirements. Imperative verbs are used in the instructions.

Answers

You will need**:**
- the children in *your* class
- a *rolled-up* newspaper
- a small box of coins
- a blindfold

1. Ask the students to <u>sit</u> in a circle on the floor.
2. **C**hoose one person to be the *guard*. **H**e/She should sit in the *middle* of the circle.
3. Blindfold the guard and *give* him/her the rolled-up newspaper. ***Place*** the box of coins in *front* of him/her.
4. Choose one person in the circle to <u>try</u> to steal the box without being *tapped* by the guard**'**s newspaper. **I**f *caught***,** he/she must return to his/her place. If he/she <u>succeeds</u>**,** he/she *becomes* the new guard.

your
rolled-up
sit
guard
middle
give
Place
front
try
tapped
caught
succeeds
becomes

1. (a) Missing punctuation is in **bold type**.

   (b) Answers will vary

2. (a) Verbs are <u>underlined</u>.

   sits – sit (line 4), tries – try (line 10), succeed – succeeds (line 13)

3. (a) Spelling errors are in *italic type*.

   your, rolled-up, guard, middle, give, Place, front, tapped, caught, becomes

   (b) (i) classes   (ii) circles   (iii) boxes

Guard the Treasure!

Read the procedure for playing a game.

You will need

- *the children in yor class*
- *a small box of coins* _____
- *a roled-up newspaper*
- *a blindfold* _____

1. Ask the students to sits in a circle on the floor. _____

2. choose one person to be the gard. he/She _____

   should sit in the midle of the circle. _____

3. Blindfold the guard and giv him/her the _____

   rolled-up newspaper. plase the box of coins in _____

   frunt of him/her. _____

4. choose one person in the circle to tries to steal _____

   the box without being taped by the guards _____

   newspaper. if cort he/she must return to _____

   his/her place. If he/she succeed he/she _____

   becumes the new guard. _____

❶ Punctuation

(a) Write the 4 missing capitals, 2 commas, 1 apostrophe to show possession and 1 colon for an offset list.

A hyphen (-) is used in some words to connect smaller words; for example, "happy-go-lucky," "self-pity," "blue-black."

(b) The word "rolled-up" in the text is hyphenated. Use a dictionary to find three more hyphenated words that contain the word "roll."

_____

_____

_____

❷ Grammar

*In any sentence, the subject and the verb have to agree in person and in number; for example, "He **sees**" but "They **see**."*

(a) Three verbs in the text do not agree with their subjects. Write the correct form of each verb in the space at the end of the line where it is found.

❸ Spelling

(a) Write the correct spelling for the misspelled words in the space at the end of each line.

You can add "s" or "es" to most words to make them plurals.

(b) Write the plural form of each of these words from the text.

(i) class _____

(ii) circle _____

(iii) box _____

Eyewitness Account

Lesson Focus

Punctuation

- Grammatical commas
- Periods
- Apostrophes to show possession

Spelling

- Misspelled words
- Confused words: their/there, were/where

Grammar

- Pronouns
- Adverbs
- Prepositions

Vocabulary

- Synonyms

Teacher Information

A recount retells events as they happened in time order. Recounts are usually written using verbs in the past tense.

Answers

I was standing <u>calmly</u> at the traffic lights at St. Lucy**'**s Square when <u>I</u> heard the sound of running footsteps a few yards behind <u>me</u>**.** I turned to see a young man <u>viciously</u> snatch an elderly woman**'**s handbag from under her arm**.** Then <u>he</u> pushed her over and kept *running***.** I raced over to the woman**,** who was struggling to her feet. As *there* was no one else in sight**,** I yelled out for help and was *relieved* to see a police officer round the corner. We <u>carefully</u> helped the woman into a nearby shop *where* the owner kindly gave <u>her</u> a glass of water**.** She recovered <u>quickly</u> and helped me to give a description of the man *who* had robbed her**.**

calmly	
I	
me	
viciously	
he	
running	
there	
relieved	
carefully	
where	
her	
quickly	
who	

1. Missing punctuation is in **bold type**.

2. Grammar answers are underlined.

   (a) Pronouns are <u>underlined</u>.

      me – I (line 2), I – me (line 3) it – he (line 5), him – her (line 11)

   (b) Adverbs are <u>**underlined in bold**</u>.

      calmly, viciously, carefully, quickly

   (c) (i) a description **of** the man

      (ii) the bag **under** her arm

3. (a) Spelling errors are in *italic type*.

      running, there, relieved, where, who

4. (a) Answers will vary, but may include the following:

      (i) attacked   (ii) shoved   (iii) sped   (iv) shouted

Eyewitness Account

Read the recount.

I was standing calm at the traffic lights at St. Lucys _____

Square when me heard the sound of running footsteps _____

a few yards behind I. I turned to see a young man _____

vicious snatch an elderly womans handbag from _____

under her arm Then it pushed her over and kept _____

runing. I raced over to the woman who was _____

struggling to her feet. As their was no one else in _____

sight I yelled out for help and was releived to see a _____

police officer round the corner. We careful _____

helped the woman into a nearby shop were the _____

owner kindly gave him a glass of water She recovered _____

quick and helped me to give a description of the _____

man hoo had robbed her _____

❶ Punctuation

(a) Find the 2 missing commas, 3 periods and 2 apostrophes to show possession.

❷ Grammar

Pronouns are words that replace nouns; for example, "I," "he," "she," "him," "it."

(a) Circle the incorrect pronouns used in the text. Write the correct pronouns in the space at the end of the line.

Adverbs are words that describe verbs. They often end in "ly"; for example, "happily," "slowly."

(b) Four words from the text are missing the "ly" ending that makes them adverbs. Write each one correctly in the space at the end of the line.

Prepositions are positional words placed before nouns and pronouns to indicate their relation to other words; for example; "He was at the traffic lights."

(c) Write the missing prepositions from the text.

　(i)　a description _____ the man

　(ii)　the bag _____ her arm

❸ Spelling

(a) Write the correct spelling for the misspelled words in the space at the end of the line.

❹ Vocabulary

(a) Write a synonym for each of these words from the text.

　(i) robbed _____

　(ii) pushed _____

　(iii) raced _____

　(iv) yelled _____

The Aquada

Lesson Focus

Punctuation

- Capital letters for sentence beginnings
- Capital letters for proper nouns
- Question marks
- Exclamation marks
- Apostrophes in contractions
- Hyphens

Spelling

- Confused words: by/buy, off/of
- Misspelled words

Grammar

- Adverbs

Vocabulary

- Compound words

Teacher Information

Descriptions describe the characteristics, components and functions of specific living or nonliving things.

Answers

Would you like to own a car that**'**s *also* a boat**?** **Y**ou can *buy* one now—but you won't get much change out *of* $500,000**!**
The **A**quada is a <u>slick-looking</u> sports car that can *seat* three people. It has all the normal car *controls*, like a speedometer and a fuel *gauge*. It doesn**'**t have any doors—you have to <u>carefully</u> climb in! **T**his is so the car is <u>completely</u> <u>watertight</u>.
If you want to go onto *water*, all you do is press a button. When the car senses it**'**s floating, it <u>quickly</u> retracts the *wheels* and lights up the navigation lights that *surround* the license plate. **T**he car is now a <u>jet-powered</u> boat**!** It can do *almost* 30 *miles* per hour at top speed.

	also
	buy
	of
	seat
	controls
	gauge
	carefully
	completely
	water
	quickly
	wheels
	surround
	almost
	miles

1. (a) Missing punctuation is in **bold type**.

   (b) (i) slick-looking

   (ii) Teacher check

2. (a) Adverbs are <u>underlined</u>.

   carefully, completely, quickly

3. (a) Spelling errors are in *italic type*.

   also, buy, of, seat, controls, gauge, water, wheels, surround, almost, miles

4. (a) Compound words are <u>underlined in bold</u>.

   slick-looking, carefully, watertight, jet-powered

   (b) carefully and watertight

The Aquada

Read the description.

would you like to own a car thats allso a boat you

can by one now – but you won't get much

change out off $500,000

The aquada *is a slick-looking sports car that can seet*

three people. It has all the normal car kontrols, like a

speedometer and a fuel gage. It doesnt have any

doors—you have to careful climb in! this is so the

car is complete watertight.

if you want to go onto warter, all you do is press a

button. When the car senses its floating, it quick

retracts the wheals and lights up the navigation lights

that suround the license plate. the car is now a

jet-powered boat It can do allmost 30

myles per hour at top speed.

_____
_____
_____
_____
_____
_____
_____
_____
_____
_____
_____
_____

❶ Punctuation

(a) Write the missing 6 capital letters, 1 question mark, 3 apostrophes and 2 exclamation marks needed for emphasis.

A hyphen (-) is used in some words to connect smaller words; for example, "happy-go-lucky," "self-pity," "able-bodied."

(b) (i) The word "jet-powered" is one of the hyphenated compound words in the text. Underline the other.

(ii) Find three hyphenated words starting with "j" in a dictionary.

❷ Grammar

Adverbs are words that describe verbs. They often end in "ly"; for example, "happily," "quickly."

(a) Write 3 adverbs that are missing the "ly" ending in the space at the end of the line.

❸ Spelling

(a) Write the correct spelling for the misspelled words in the space at the end of the line.

❹ Vocabulary

Compound words are made up of two smaller words; for example, "rainbow."

(a) Circle the compound words in the text.

(b) Which 2 are unhyphenated?

_____

Playhouse

Lesson Focus

Punctuation

- Capital letters for proper nouns
- Capital letters for sentence beginnings
- Periods
- Commas in lists
- Grammatical commas
- Quotation marks for direct speech

Spelling

- Misspelled words

Grammar

- Adverbs

Vocabulary

- Compound words

Teacher Information

Narratives tell a story, often involving fictitious characters, in a sequence of events.

Answers

Jack *swung* open the door of the old <u>playhouse</u> and stepped <u>inside</u>. **I**t *slammed* shut <u>behind</u> him. He *stared* <u>around</u> with wide eyes.
In the middle of the room**,** in the *thick* dust and spider webs, stood a small *wooden* table. It was set with polished silver plates and *cutlery* and a single candle was burning <u>brightly</u> in an elaborate <u>candlestick</u>**.** **J**ack shivered <u>violently</u>. This was *creepy*. And the damp**,** musty smell was making him feel *queasy*. He had to get out.
<u>Swiftly</u>**,** he turned <u>toward</u> the door and *grabbed* at the handle.
"Don**'**t go. Come and eat**,**" *whispered* a *voice* in his ear.
Jack screamed and <u>desperately</u> rattled the handle.
"Help! **L**et me *out*!**"**

swung	
slammed	
stared	
thick	
wooden	
cutlery	
brightly	
violently	
creepy	
queasy	
Swiftly	
grabbed	
whispered	
voice	
desperately	
out	

1. Missing punctuation is in **bold type**.
2. (a) Adverbs are <u>underlined</u>.
   brightly, violently, Swiftly, desperately
3. (a) Spelling errors are in *italic type*.
   swung, slammed, stared, thick, wooden, cutlery, creepy, queasy, grabbed, whispered, voice, out
4. Compound words are <u>**underlined in bold**</u>.
   (a) playhouse, candlestick

Playhouse

Read the narrative.

Jack swunng open the door of the old playhouse
and stepped inside it slamed shut behind him. He
starred around with wide eyes.

In the middle of the room in the thic dust and
spider webs, stood a small woodden table. It was
set with polished silver plates and cutelry and a
single candle was burning **with brightness** in an
elaborate candlestick jack shivered **with violence**.

This was kreepy. And the damp musty smell was
making him feel queazy. He had to get out.

With swiftness he turned toward the door and
grabed at the handle.

Dont go. Come and eat" wisppered a
voyce in his ear.

Jack screamed and **with desperation** rattled the handle.

Help! let me owt!

_____
_____
_____
_____
_____
_____
_____
_____
_____
_____
_____
_____
_____
_____

❶ Punctuation

(a) Find the missing 3 capital letters, 2
periods, 4 commas and 1 apostrophe.

*The actual words spoken by a person are
called direct speech. These begin and end
with quotation marks.*

(b) Write the missing quotation marks from
the direct speech in the text.

❷ Grammar

*Adverbs are words that describe verbs. They
often end in "ly"; for example, "happily,"
"slowly."*

(a) Look at the words in bold type in the text.
Replace each group of words with one
adverb with the same meaning. Write
each one in the space at the end of the
line.

❸ Spelling

(a) Write the misspelled words correctly in
the space at the end of the line.

❹ Vocabulary

*Compound words are made up of two smaller
words; for example, "rainbow."*

(a) Write 2 compound words used in the
text.

_____

Birthday Parties

Lesson Focus

Punctuation

- Grammatical commas
- Question marks
- Apostrophes to show possession

Grammar

- Subject-verb agreement

Spelling

- Misspelled words
- Confused words: there/their, too/to

Vocabulary

- Antonyms

Writing

- Paragraphs

Teacher Information

A report is usually written in the present tense and provides facts clearly without unnecessary information or opinions.

Answers

Have you ever wondered why we <u>celebrate</u> birthdays with *parties***?**	celebrate
	parties
Long ago in Europe**,** people thought that evil *spirits* were *attracted* to people on their birthdays. To protect them**,** friends and family would <u>gather</u> to bring their good *wishes* and gifts for the birthday person. At first, only kings celebrated *their* birthdays, but soon people began *to* celebrate children**'**s birthdays *too*.	spirits
	attracted
	gather
	wishes
	their
	to
	too
Many children**'**s birthday parties include games. A lot of *these* games involve the unknown, such as "Pin the Tail on the Donkey" or "Musical *Chairs*." Traditionally**,** they <u>symbolize</u> the unknown in the new year of life that *lies* ahead for the birthday child.	Many
	these
	chairs
	symbolize
	lies

1. Missing punctuation is in **bold type**.

2. (a) Verbs are <u>underlined</u>.

    celebrates – celebrate (line 1), gathers – gather (line 5), symbolizes – symbolize (line 13)

3. (a) Spelling errors are in *italic type*.

    parties, spirits, attracted, wishes, their, to, too, Many, these, chairs, lies

4. (a) Possible answers:

    (i) good   (ii) neglect/destroy/harm

5. Teacher check

Birthday Parties

Read the report.

Have you ever wondered why we celebrates
_____

birthdays with partys
_____

Long ago in Europe people thought that evil spirrits
_____

were attrackted to people on their birthdays. To
_____

protect them friends and family would gathers
_____

to bring their good wishs and gifts for the birthday
_____

person. At first, only kings celebrated there birthdays,
_____

but soon people began too celebrate childrens
_____

birthdays to.
_____

Manny childrens birthday parties include games.
_____

A lot of theese games involve the unknown, such as
_____

"Pin the Tail on the Donkey" or "Musical Chaires."
_____

Traditionally they symbolizes the unknown in the new
_____

year of life that lyse ahead for the birthday child.
_____

❶ Punctuation

(a) Find 3 missing commas, 1 question mark and 2 apostrophes.

❷ Grammar

In any sentence, the subject and the verb have to agree in person and in number; for example, "He **sees**" but "They **see**."

(a) Three verbs in the text do not agree with their subjects. Circle them and write the correct form of each verb in the space at the end of the line.

❸ Spelling

(a) Write the misspelled words correctly in the space at the end of the line.

❹ Vocabulary

(a) Write an antonym (a word with the opposite meaning) for these words from the text.

(i) evil _____

(ii) protect _____

❺ Writing

The first paragraph states what the report is about.

(a) Write a question answered by paragraphs 2 and 3.

Paragraph 2. _____

_____

_____

Paragraph 3 _____

_____

_____

Be Healthy! Be Happy!

Lesson Focus

Punctuation

- Capital letters for sentence beginnings
- Periods
- Commas for lists
- Apostrophes in grammatical contractions

Grammar

- Adjectives

Spelling

- Misspelled words
- Confused words – of/off, rays/raise, too/two
- Plurals – "s," "es," changing "y" to "i" to add "es"

Vocabulary

- Antonyms

Teacher Information

Expositions present one side of an argument to persuade the reader to a particular point of view.

Answers

We need to improve our <u>lifestyles</u>.	Capital letter
The car**,** TV and fast <u>foods</u> are turning	Comma
us into a nation *of* unhealthy, unfit people.	of
More *people* suffer from diet-related <u>illnesses</u>	people
than ever *before* as a result of regularly	before
eating <u>meals</u> high in fat and sugar**.** Young	Period
people need to *learn* the importance of eating	learn
healthy food to prevent medical <u>problems</u>.	healthy
TV**,** <u>DVDs</u> and computer <u>games</u> are becoming	Comma
the most popular *leisure* <u>activities</u> for many	leisure
young people. **M**ore time needs to be spent	Capital letter
enjoying physical <u>activities</u> that *raise* the	raise
heart rate and make the body work harder**.**	Period
We are relying *too* much on the car for transport.	too
There must be <u>times</u> when we can walk instead.	Capital letter
If we look after our *<u>bodies</u>* they will work well for us.	bodies
Let**'**s do it!	Apostrophe

1. (a) Missing punctuation is in **bold type**.

2. (a) (i) fast <u>foods</u>   (ii) medical <u>problems</u>   (iii) popular <u>activities</u>

   (iv) physical <u>activities</u>

3. (a) Spelling errors are in *italic type*.

   of, people, before, learn, healthy, leisure, raise, too, bodies

   (b) Plural nouns are <u>underlined</u>.

   "s" – lifestyles, foods, meals, problems, DVDs, games, times

   "es" – illnesses

   "ies" – activities, bodies

4. (a) Possible answers include:

   (i) unpopular   (ii) work   (iii) irregularly, sometimes

Be Healthy! Be Happy!

Read the exposition.

we need to improve our lifestyles.

The car TV and fast foods are turning

us into a nation off unhealthy, unfit people.

More peeple suffer from diet-related illnesses

than ever befour as a result of regularly

eating meals high in fat and sugar Young

people need to lurn the importance of eating

hellthy food to prevent medical problems.

TV DVDs and computer games are becoming

the most popular leshure activities for many

young people. more time needs to be spent

enjoying physical activities that rays the

heart rate and make the body work harder

We are relying two much on the car for transport.

there must be times when we can walk instead.

If we look after our body's they will work well for us.

Lets do it!

---

❶ Punctuation
(a) Underline the 8 punctuation mistakes in the text and write the correction in the space at the end of the line.

❷ Grammar
   Adjectives describe nouns.
(a) Find the nouns in the text described by these adjectives.

   (i) fast   (ii) medical

   _____   _____

   (iii) popular   (iv) physical

   _____   _____

❸ Spelling
(a) There are 9 misspelled words. Underline each and write it correctly in the space at the end of the line.

The plural of words is made in different ways: by adding "s," "es" or, if the word ends in "y," it is changed to "i" before "es" is added; for example, "boot(s)," "match(es)," "ladies" ("y" to "i" and add "es").

(b) Underline all the plural nouns in the text using a different color for each of the 3 different ways the plural is made.

❹ Vocabulary
(a) Write an antonym (a word with the opposite meaning) for each of these words from the text.

   (i)   popular _____

   (ii) leisure _____

   (iii) regularly _____

The Ballad of Ned Kelly

Lesson Focus

Punctuation

- Capital letter at the beginning of each line of a poem
- Capital letter for proper nouns

Grammar

- Adjectives

Spelling

- Misspelled words
- "i" before "e"

Teacher Information

Ballads are narratives that tell stories of heroes and folk tales. They may be sung or recited, often include rhyming couplets and contain a repeated line.

Answers

1. Missing punctuation is in **bold type**.
   (b) Proper nouns are underlined.
      Irish, Ned, Kelly, Ned, Fitzpatrick, Mrs, Kelly, Ned, Ned, Kelly, Gang, June, Ned, Kelly, November, Ned's

2. (a) (i) stolen horse
      (ii) poor parents or Irish parents
      (iii) hangman's rope
      (iv) bushranger legend

3. (a) Spelling errors are in *italic type*.
      (i) receiving
      (ii) pierced
   (b) * "i" before "e" except after "c," is the spelling rule.

An **I**rish lad named **N**ed **K**elly
Was born in 1854.
His parents worked from dawn to dusk
But still were very poor.
But still were very poor.

When **N**ed was twelve his father died
And life got even worse.
At sixteen years he went to jail
For *receiving* a stolen horse.
For *receiving* a stolen horse.

An argument with a policeman
(**F**itzpatrick was his name)
Sent **M**rs **K**elly away for three years
And then **N**ed rose to fame.
Then **N**ed rose to fame.

The bush became his second home
And when one day, by chance
He came upon some policemen,
He finally took a stance.
He finally took a stance.

The **K**elly **G**ang shot them dead
And robbery became their trade.
No rich man's bank was safe from them
And a legend had been made.
A legend had been made.

June 1880 will be remembered
As **N**ed **K**elly's last stand,
Dressed in armor made of steel
With shotgun in his hand.
Shotgun in his hand.

His comrades fell and still he fought
Relentless to the last.
More than twenty-eight bullets *pierced* his skin
And so the die was cast.
So the die was cast.

In **N**ovember 1880, at twenty-eight,
Ned's life came to an end.
A hangman's rope sealed the fate
Of our bushranger legend.
Our bushranger legend.

The Ballad of Ned Kelly

Read the ballad.

an irish lad named ned kelly
was born in 1854.
his parents worked from dawn to dusk
but still were very poor.
but still were very poor.

when ned was twelve his father died
and life got even worse.
at sixteen years he went to jail
for recieving a stolen horse.
for recieving a stolen horse.

an argument with a policeman
(fitzpatrick was his name)
sent mrs kelly away for three years
and then ned rose to fame.
then ned rose to fame.

the bush became his second home
and when one day, by chance
he came upon some policemen,
he finally took a stance.
he finally took a stance.

the kelly gang shot them dead
and robbery became their trade.
no rich man's bank was safe from them
and a legend had been made.
a legend had been made.

june 1880 will be remembered
as ned kelly's last stand,
dressed in armor made of steel
with shotgun in his hand.
shotgun in his hand.

his comrades fell and still he fought
relentless to the last.
more than twenty-eight bullets peirced
his skin
and so the die was cast.
so the die was cast.

in november 1880, at twenty-eight,
ned's life came to an end.
a hangman's rope sealed the fate
of our bushranger legend.
our bushranger legend.

❶ Punctuation

The beginning of each line of a poem generally begins with a capital letter.

(a) Circle the word at the beginning of each line which needs a capital letter.

(b) Underline 16 proper nouns which need a capital letter.

❷ Grammar

(a) Find and write adjectives to match these nouns:

(i) horse _____

(ii) parents _____

(iii) rope _____

(iv) legend _____

❸ Spelling

(a) There are 2 misspelled words. Write the correct spelling.

(i) recieving _____

(ii) peirced _____

(b) Write the spelling rule.

Art Thief Arrest

Lesson Focus

Punctuation

- Capital letters for proper nouns
- Apostrophes to show possession
- Quotation marks for direct speech

Grammar

- Verb tenses
- Pronouns

Spelling

- Confused words: one/won
- Misspelled words

Writing

- Double negatives

Teacher Information

A recount retells events as they happened, in time order. Recounts are written using verbs in the past tense.

Answers

> Art *thief* Winston Rose has *finally* been arrested after having been chased by the world's police for more than ten years. The details of his amazing *escapes* can be found in **W**illiam Green's book, **_Artful Dodging_**. The infamous criminal has stolen *priceless* paintings from *museums* and art galleries in 12 countries. Rose's method was to cut a painting out of its frame and replace it with a picture of a red rose.
> **R**ose is *known* as an expert at avoiding security alarms, but yesterday he set *one* off as he entered the Franklin Gallery in **L**ondon.
> **"**I think Rose is as *surprised* as we are about the alarm,**"** said a *police* spokesperson yesterday. "**He** is now in custody but is not saying anything about what he has done with all the *stolen* art.**"**

1. Missing punctuation is in **bold type**.

2. (a) Verbs are <u>underlined.</u>

    Answers will vary, but should include four of the following:
    been arrested, having been chased, has stolen, was to cut, was set (off), entered, has done

   (b) Pronouns are shaded gray.

    him – his (line 2), their – its (line 6), she – he (line 8), Him – He (line 10)

3. Spelling errors are in *italic type*.

    thief, finally, escapes, priceless, museums, known, one, surprised, police, stolen

4. (a) One way of correcting the double negative has been <u>**underlined in bold**</u>.

    "…is not saying nothing" should read "…is not saying anything" or "…is saying nothing."

Art Thief Arrest

Read the newspaper report.

Art theif Winston Rose has finaly been arrested after having been chased by the worlds police for more than ten years. The details of him amazing excapes can be found in william Greens book, <u>artful dodging</u>.

The infamous criminal has stolen priceles paintings from musuems and art galleries in 12 countries. Roses method was to cut a painting out of their frame and replace it with a picture of a red rose.

rose is nown as an expert at avoiding security alarms, but yesterday he set won off as she entered the Franklin Gallery in london.

I think Rose is as suprised as we are about the alarm, said a pollice spokesperson yesterday. "Him is now in custody, but is not saying nothing about what he has done with all the stollen art."

❶ Punctuation

(a) Write the 5 missing capital letters and 3 apostrophes to show possession.

   Quotation marks show what a person is saying.

(b) Add the quotation marks missing from the text.

❷ Grammar

*Verbs written in the past tense show what has already happened; for example, "He **went** to the shops," "Michael **wrote** a story," "She **washed** the dishes."*

(a) Write four past tense verbs from the text.

Pronouns are words that replace nouns; for example, "I," "he," "she," "him," "it," "her," "them," "my."

(b) Circle the incorrect pronouns used in the text. Above each, write the pronoun that should have been used.

❸ Spelling

(a) Write the correct spelling of the 10 misspelled words.

_____

_____

_____

_____

_____

❹ Writing

*A double negative statement incorrectly uses two negative words; for example, "I **haven't** got **no** more," should be "I haven't any more" or "I have no more."*

(a) Underline the line in the text containing a double negative. Write it correctly.

The Titanic Should Be Left Alone

Lesson Focus

Punctuation

- Commas in a list
- Grammatical commas
- Periods
- Apostrophes for possession
- Apostrophes in contractions

Grammar

- Verb tenses

Spelling

- Confused words: allowed/aloud
- Misspelled words

Vocabulary

- Synonyms
- Compound words

Teacher Information

An exposition evaluates an issue. Arguments are given to persuade the audience to a particular point of view.

Answers

> The Titanic was a large**,** luxurious ship that sank in 1912**,** taking 1513 people with it**.** The wreck <u>was</u> found in 1985. Since that time, *thousands* of artifacts have been taken from the Titanic. Some people think this is *wrong***.** They say the Titanic is really a <u>graveyard</u> and should be left alone.
>
> I don**'**t think that just <u>anyone</u> should be *allowed* to visit the <u>shipwreck</u>. But if *scientists* are careful**,** I can**'**t see <u>anything</u> wrong with *removing* artifacts from the Titanic**.** People can then go to see them in museums. This is a good way to pay our respects to the people who <u>died</u> in the disaster. If the artifacts are left <u>underwater</u>, they will *eventually* perish and no one will ever see them**.** I think that**'**s a shame. The people who died on the Titanic must be *remembered***.** Bringing the ship**'**s artifacts to the *surface* is the best way to do this.

1. Missing punctuation is in **bold type**.

2. (a) Verbs are <u>underlined</u>.

     will be – was (line 2), will die – died (line 8)

3. (a) Spelling errors are in *italic type*.

     thousands, wrong, allowed, scientists, removing, eventually, remembered, surface

4. (a) Answers will vary, but may include the following:

     (i) deteriorate, decompose

     (ii) calamity, catastrophe

   (b) Compound words have been <u>**underlined in bold**</u>.

     anyone, anything, graveyard, shipwreck, underwater

   (c) Teacher check

The Titanic Should Be Left Alone

Read the exposition.

The Titanic was a large luxurious ship that sank in 1912 taking 1513 people with it The wreck will be found in 1985. Since that time, thouzands of artifacts have been taken from the Titanic. Some people think this is rong They say the Titanic is really a graveyard and should be left alone.

I dont think that just anyone should be aloud to visit the shipwreck. But if sientists are careful I cant see anything wrong with remooving artefacts from the Titanic People can then go to see them in museums. This is a good way to pay our respects to the people who will die in the disaster. If the artifacts are left underwater, they will eventualy perish and no one will ever see them I think thats a shame. The people who died on the Titanic must be remembed Bringing the ships artifacts to the surfase is the best way to do this.

① Punctuation

(a) Find the 1 comma missing from a list, 2 grammatical commas, 5 periods, 3 apostrophes for contractions and 1 apostrophe for possession.

② Grammar

*Verbs in the future tense describe what will happen in the future. The word "will" can be used to show this; for example, "He **will** go," "She **will** see."*

(a) Two of the verbs in the text have been written in the future tense. Circle them and write the correct verb tense above each.

③ Spelling

(a) Write the correct spelling of the 8 misspelled words.

_____

_____

_____

④ Vocabulary

(a) Use a thesaurus or dictionary to write synonyms for these words from the text.

(i) perish _____

(ii) disaster _____

Compound words are made up of two smaller words; for example, "rainbow."

(b) Write 4 compound words found in this text.

(c) Write 5 compound words (hyphenated or unhyphenated) with the words "ship" or "water." Use a dictionary.

_____

_____

_____

The Marine Turtle

Lesson Focus

Punctuation

- Capital letters for sentence beginnings
- Periods
- Grammatical commas
- Hyphens

Grammar

- Conjunctions

Spelling

- Confused words: through/threw, there/their, sun/son, ate/eight, prey/pray
- Misspelled words

Teacher Information

A report is usually written in the present tense and provides facts clearly and without unnecessary information or opinions.

Answers

> **T**he turtle is a reptile**,** a <u>cold-blooded</u> animal that breathes air *through* its lungs**.** **T**he main feature of the turtle is its hard shell, which can be up to a *meter* in *length***.**
>
> *There* are seven types of marine turtle**,** most of them living in the warm tropical oceans, where they feed on algae and sea grasses**.**
>
> **T**urtles spend most of their time in the water, but the female crawls on to the beach to lay her <u>rubbery-shelled</u> eggs**.** **S**he digs a hole in the sand and lays as many as two hundred eggs**.** **T**he eggs are covered with sand for protection from the *sun* and *predators***.** **A**fter about *eight* weeks**,** they are ready to hatch**.**
>
> **M**ost young turtles fail to reach the ocean as the trip across the open sand is a dangerous one**.** *Young* turtles are easy *prey* for birds and other animals**.**

1. (a) Missing punctuation is in **bold type**.

    (b) Hyphenated words are <u>underlined.</u>

    cold-blooded, rubbery-shelled

    (c) (i) self-service   (ii) mini-mart   (iii) half-hearted   (iv) sea-dog

2. (a) Answers should include the following:

    that, which, where, but, and, as

3. (a) Spelling errors are in *italic type*.

    through, meter, length, there, sun, predators, eight, young, prey

The Marine Turtle

Read the report.

the turtle is a reptile a cold-blooded animal that breathes air threw its lungs the main feature of the turtle is its hard shell, which can be up to a metre in lenth

their are seven types of marine turtle most of them living in the warm tropical oceans where they feed on algae and sea grasses

turtles spend most of their time in the water, but the female crawls on to the beach to lay her rubbery-shelled eggs she digs a hole in the sand and lays as many as two hundred eggs the eggs are covered with sand for protection from the son and preditors after about ate weeks they are ready to hatch

most young turtles fail to reach the ocean as the trip across the open sand is a dangerous one yung turtles are easy pray for birds and other animals

❶ Punctuation

(a) Write in 9 capital letters, 9 periods and 3 grammatical commas.

A hyphen (-) is used in some words to connect smaller words; for example, "do-it-yourself," "weight-lifter" and "well-presented."

(b) Circle the 2 hyphenated words in the text.

(c) Make hyphenated words from the list below to match each definition.

mini	hearted	sea	service
dog	half	self	mart

(i)   customers serve themselves

_____

(ii) small supermarket

_____

(iii) showing little enthusiasm

_____

(iv) experienced sailor

_____

❷ Grammar

Conjunctions are words that join single words or groups of words to make a sentence longer.

(a) Write 3 conjunctions used in the text.

❸ Spelling

(a) Highlight the 9 misspelled words in the report, then write the correct spelling below.

_____

_____

_____

_____

Matthew's Story

Lesson Focus

Punctuation

- Grammatical commas
- Apostrophes to show possession
- Colons in titles

Grammar

- Adverbs
- Adjectives

Spelling

- Misspelled words
- Confused words: herd/heard, right/write/rite

Teacher Information

An autobiography is a type of recount. A recount retells events as they happened in time order. Recounts are usually written using verbs in the past tense.

Answers

My Life: The Story of Matthew Marsh

I was born in London in 1967. My family's main *interest*	interest
was sports and my parents <u>actively</u>	actively
encouraged me to play team sports from an	encouraged
early age. But I really didn't enjoy playing sports. I	early
preferred to play my violin.	preferred
When I left school, I found a job as a baker's *assistant*	assistant
and kept practicing my violin. One day**,** I *heard* that	heard
a new music group was looking for a *violinist*. I called	violinist
and <u>nervously</u> auditioned for the	nervously
group's lead *singer* the next day. To my delight**,** I got in.	singer
I *enjoyed* the band's music and spent the next	enjoyed
few years <u>happily</u> playing electric violin. When	happily
the band broke up in 1997**,** I started to *write* my own	write
pop music. My songs have been *performed* by	performed
some of the world's most *famous* singers. I now live in	famous
Los Angeles where I *work* in my home studio.	work

1. Missing punctuation is in **bold type**.

2. (a) Adverbs are <u>underlined</u>.

    actively, nervously, happily

   (b) Answers should include three of the following:

    main, team, early, baker's, new, music, lead, next, few, electric, own, pop, famous, home

3. (a) Spelling errors are in *italic type*.

    interest, encouraged, early, preferred, assistant, heard, violinist, singer, enjoyed, write, performed, famous, work

Matthew's Story

Read the autobiography.

My Life The Story of Matthew Marsh

I was born in London in 1967. My familys main intrest

was sports and my parents **with activeness**

enckouraged me to play team sports from an

urly age. But I really didn't enjoy playing sports. I

preffered to play my violin.

_____

When I left school, I found a job as a bakers asistent

and kept practicing my violin. One day I herd that

a new music group was looking for a voilinist. I called

and **with nervousness** auditioned for the

groups lead singger the next day. To my delight I got in.

_____

I ennjoyed the bands music and spent the next

few years **with happiness** playing electric violin. When

the band broke up in 1997 I started to rite my own

pop music. My songs have been perfformmed by

some of the worlds most famus singers. I now live in

Los Angeles where I werk in my home studio.

_____

❶ Punctuation

(a) Find the 3 missing commas and 5 apostrophes to show possession. Correct the title by adding the missing colon.

❷ Grammar

Adverbs are words that describe verbs. They often end in "ly"; for example, "happily," "slowly."

(a) Look at the words in bold print in the text. Replace each group of words with one adverb with the same meaning. Write each one in the space at the end of the line.

*Adjectives are words that describe nouns; for example, **red** car, **juicy** apple.*

(b) Write 3 adjectives you can find in the text.

❸ Spelling

(a) Write the misspelled words correctly in the space at the end of the line.

The Great Barrier Reef

Lesson Focus

Punctuation

- Capital letters for sentence beginnings
- Capital letters for proper nouns
- Periods
- Grammatical commas

Grammar

- Subject-verb agreement
- Prepositions

Spelling

- Confused words: they're/their
- Misspelled words

Vocabulary

- Enrichment

Teacher Information

This description describes the physical characteristics and special features of the Great Barrier Reef.

Answers

> **T**he **G**reat **B**arrier **R**eef is the largest coral reef in the *world*. **I**t is nearly 1450 miles long and <u>stretches</u> along most of the northeastern coastline of **A**ustralia**.**
>
> *A*lthough the reef is so large**,** it <u>is</u> actually made of very small coral polyps and algae**.** **T**he hard part of the reef is made from the *skeletons* of these small creatures**.**
>
> **C**oral polyps <u>are</u> not**,** as they appear**,** members of the plant family**,** but are really small *animals* that have poisonous tentacles**.** **T**hese animals feed on *plankton* and when they die *their skeletons* remain**.**

Answers

1. Missing punctuation is in **bold type**.

2. (a) Verbs are <u>underlined</u>.

   stretch – stretches (line 2), are – is (line 3), is – are (line 5)

   (b) (i) were   (ii) want   (iii) is   (iv) has

   (c) (i) in   (ii) along   (iii) from

3. (a) Spelling errors are in *italic type*.

   world, Although, skeletons, animals, plankton, their, skeletons

4. (a) largest – most extensive, long – in length, large – vast, very small – tiny, hard – solid, poisonous – venomous, feed – feast

The Great Barrier Reef

Read the description.

the great barrier reef is the **largest** coral reef in the wurld it is nearly 1450 miles **long** and stretch along most of the northeastern coastline of australia

althow the reef is so **large** it are actually made of **very small** coral polyps and algae the **hard** part of the reef is made from the skelertons of these small creatures

coral polyps is not as they appear members of the plant family but are really small aminals that have **poisonous** tentacles these animals **feed** on plancton and when they die they're skelingtons remain

❶ Punctuation

(a) Find the 10 missing capital letters, 6 periods and 4 commas.

❷ Grammar

*The subject and verb must always agree in person and in number. For example; "she **swims**," but "we **swim**."*

(a) In the text, circle the 3 verbs that do not agree with their subjects. Write the correction above each word.

(b) Circle the verbs below that agree with their subjects.

  (i) The children was/were interested in marine science.

  (ii) They wants/want to see the Great Barrier Reef.

  (iii) It is/are under threat.

  (iv) It has/have to be protected.

*Prepositions are positional words placed before nouns and pronouns to indicate their relation to other words; for example, "I had my shower **after** dinner," "My mother is proud **of** me."*

(c) Write the missing prepositions from the text.

  (i) the largest coral reef _____ the world

  (ii) it stretches _____ the northeastern coastline.

  (iii) the reef is made _____ the skeletons of coral polyps.

❸ Spelling

(a) Underline the 7 spelling errors and write the correction above each word.

❹ Vocabulary

A good choice of vocabulary can make a piece of writing more interesting.

in length	tiny	feast	solid
most extensive		vast	venomous

(a) Replace the bold words or phrases in the text with those from the list above. Write the new words or phrases above the originals.

Hermes

Lesson Focus

Punctuation

- Capital letters for sentence beginnings
- Capital letters for proper nouns
- Periods
- Grammatical commas
- Apostrophes for possession

Spelling

- Misspelled words

Grammar

- Indefinite articles (a/an)
- Prepositions

Teacher Information

A narrative tells a story in a sequence of events. This narrative is in the form of a fable.

Answers

Hermes was the son of the god **Z**eus and <u>a mountain</u> nymph**.**	a
He was a very *special* child who**,** on his first day of life**,** found	special
<u>an empty</u> tortoise shell and used it to make the first musical	an
instrument**,** <u>a lyre</u>**.**	a
Hermes was known for his *helpfulness* to humanity**. W**hen	helpfulness
Perseus was *ordered* by the king to bring him **M**edusa**'**s head	ordered
as a gift**, H**ermes provided him with <u>a helmet</u> to make him	a
invisible and magic sandals so that he could fly swiftly**. P**erseus	invisible
was able to complete his mission *successfully***,** thanks to the	successfully
assistance **H**ermes had given**.**	assistance
As the patron of *travelers***,** it was **H**ermes**'**s job to convey dead	travellers
souls to the underworld**.**	souls
Hermes was also the messenger of the gods**. H**e carried <u>a</u>	a
<u>special</u> staff and is often depicted wearing <u>a straw</u> hat**.**	a

1. Missing punctuation is in **bold type**.

2. (a) A/An words are <u>underlined.</u>

    a mountain, an empty, a lyre, a helmet, a special, a straw

   (b) (i) an urgent message   (ii) a helpful hint

       (iii) an original painting   (iv) a useful appliance

       (v) an honest mistake   (vi) a one-hit wonder

   (c) (i) by   (ii) with

3. (a) Spelling errors are in *italic type.*

    special, helpfulness, ordered, invisible, successfully, assistance, travelers, souls

Hermes

Read the fable.

hermes was the son of the god zeus and an mountain nymph _____

he was a very speshal child who on his first day of life found _____

a empty tortoise shell and used it to make the first musical _____

instrament an lyre _____

hermes was known for his helpfullness to humanity when _____

perseus was ordored by the king to bring him medusas head _____

as a gift hermes provided him with an helmet to make him _____

invisable and magic sandals so that he could fly swiftly perseus _____

was able to complete his mission succesfuly thanks to the _____

asisstance hermes had given _____

as the patron of travellers it was hermess job to convey dead _____

soles to the underworld _____

hermes was also the mesenger of the gods he carried an _____

special staff and is often depicted wearing an straw hat _____

❶ Punctuation

(a) Find the missing capital letters, periods, 6 commas and 2 apostrophes.

❷ Grammar

*When the word "a" is needed before a word beginning with a vowel sound, it is necessary to change it to "an" to make it easier to say; for example, "**an** apple."*

(a) Underline 6 errors in the text where "a" and "an" have been confused. Write the correct word on the line at the end of the row.

Note: Some words beginning with the letter "h" need "an" because the "h" is silent, so the word starts with a vowel sound; for example, "an hour."

(b) Choose "a" or "an" for the following phrases.

(i) _____ urgent message

(ii) _____ helpful hint

(iv) _____ useful appliance

(iii) _____ original painting

(v) _____ honest mistake

(vi) _____ one-hit wonder

*Prepositions are positional words placed before nouns and pronouns to indicate their relation to other words; for example, "I went to bed **after** dinner," "My mother is worried **about** me."*

(c) Write the missing prepositions from the text.

(i) Perseus was ordered _____ the king

(ii) Hermes provided him _____ a helmet

❸ Spelling

(a) Write the correct spelling of 8 misspelled words on the line at the end of the row.

School Vending Machine

Lesson Focus

Punctuation

- Capital letters for sentence beginnings
- Periods
- Grammatical commas
- Apostrophes in contractions

Grammar

- Conjunctions

Spelling

- Confused words: by/buy/bye, which/witch, sew/so, there/their, some/sum
- Misspelled words
- Plurals ("s" and "es")

Writing

- Double negatives

Teacher Information

An exposition evaluates an issue. Arguments are given to persuade the audience to a particular point of view.

Answers

I think it's a good idea that our school has *decided*	decided
to *buy* a food vending machine for the	buy
<u>students</u> to use. **I**t will raise money for the school**,**	students
which will directly benefit the students.	which
Also**,** there <u>isn't a</u> cafeteria or *restaurant* at the school	restaurant
so students can't buy food from anywhere else**.**	so
This means that parents must prepare <u>sandwiches</u>	sandwiches
or other food for *their* children every day.	their
In addition**,** the school board has *promised* that the	promised
vending machine will contain only *healthy* food.	healthy
Therefore**,** **I** can't understand why *some*	some
<u>parents</u> don't want the vending machine**.** I	parents
hope it arrives soon.	hope

1. Missing punctuation is in **bold type**.

2. (a) cafeteria **or** restaurant

    sandwiches **or** other food

3. (a) buy, which, so, their, some

   (b) Spelling errors are in *italic type*.

     decided, restaurant, promised, healthy, hope

   (c) Singular nouns are <u>underlined in bold</u>.

     students (line 3), sandwiches (line 7), parents (line 12)

4. (a) One way of correcting the double negative has been <u>underlined</u>.

    "…there isn't no cafeteria or restaurant …" should read "…there isn't a cafeteria or restaurant …" or "…there is no cafeteria or restaurant …"

School Vending Machine

Read the exposition.

I think its a good idea that our school has decidded

to (by, buy, bye) a food vending machine for the

student to use it will raise money for the school

(which, witch) will directly benefit the students.

also there isn't no cafeteria or restarant at the school

(sew, so) students cant buy food from anywhere else

this means that parents must prepare sandwich

or other food for (there, their) children every day.

In addition the school board has promissed that the

vending machine will contain only hellthy food.

Therefore i cant understand why (some, sum)

parent dont want the vending machine I

hop it arrives soon.

_____ (×13)

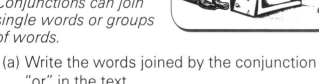

❶ Punctuation

(a) Write the missing capital letters, periods, 4 commas and 3 apostrophes.

❷ Grammar

Conjunctions can join single words or groups of words.

(a) Write the words joined by the conjunction "or" in the text.

_____

_____

❸ Spelling

(a) Choose the correct spelling from each pair of words in brackets. Write your choice in the space at the end of the line.

(b) Write the correct spelling for the misspelled words in the space.

You can add "s" or "es" to most singular nouns to make them plurals.

(c) There are 3 singular nouns in the text which need "s" or "es" added to them to make them plurals. Circle each and write its correct plural form in the space at the end of the line.

_____

_____

_____

❹ Writing

A double negative statement incorrectly uses two negative words; for example, "I haven't got no more," should be "I haven't any more" or "I have no more."

(a) Underline the words in the text containing a double negative. Write them correctly.

_____

_____

Annie the Witch

Lesson Focus

Punctuation

- Quotation marks for direct speech
- Exclamation marks
- Hyphens
- Apostrophes in grammatical contractions
- Capital letters for proper nouns

Spelling

- Misspelled words

Grammar

- Verb tense – past, present, future

Teacher Information

A narrative tells about a series of events, usually involving fictitious characters.

Answers

> "You're crazy, **M**ike**!** Old **A**nnie's a witch—everyone knows that**!"**
>
> "Rubbish, **I**an**!** My mom and dad say she's just a *lonely* old lady."
>
> "I'm telling you she's a witch**!"**
>
> **I**an shook his head, his eyes behind the thick lenses opened wide and round. He dropped his voice to a *whisper*.
>
> "And she killed her husband—she served him *poisoned* cookies and milk. Homemade chocolate chip cookies. And you want to go there by yourself—you're a nutcase**!"**
>
> But nothing could shake **M**ike.
>
> "I'm going to weed her garden for her—and she's going to pay me ten dollars. And when I have that ten dollars, I'll have saved *enough* for a new engine for my model airplane. And if you're very lucky, I might let you play with it sometimes.**"**
>
> "Yeah, if you're alive, you mean …**"**

1. Missing punctuation is in **bold type**.

   (d) Teacher check

   (f) you are, Annie is, she is, I am, I will

2. (a) Spelling errors are in *italic type*.

   lonely, whisper, poisoned, enough

3. (a) (i) knows – present   (ii) shook – past   (iii) dropped – past

   (iv) am going to weed – future

Annie the Witch

Read this narrative.

Youre crazy, mike Old annies a witch—everyone knows that

Rubbish, ian My mom and dad say shes just a lonley old lady.

Im telling you shes a witch

ian shook his head, his eyes behind the thick lenses opened wide and round. He dropped his voice to a wisper.

And she killed her husband—she served him poisned cookies and milk. Homemade chocolate chip cookies. And you want to go there by yourself—youre a nutcase

But nothing could shake mike.

Im going to weed her garden for her—and shes going to pay me ten dollars. And when I have that ten dollars, Ill have saved enugh for a new engine for my model airplane. And if youre very lucky, I might let you play with it sometimes.

Yeah, if youre alive, you mean …

❶ Punctuation

Speech marks are put at the beginning and end of what has been spoken.

(a) There are 6 separate speeches in the text. Add the missing speech marks.

(b) Write in 5 missing exclamation marks where the sentence suggests strong feelings.

(c) Find 5 capital letters needed for proper nouns.

A hyphen (-) is used in some compound words to connect smaller words; for example, choc-chip.

(d) Use a dictionary to find three other words associated with food that also use a hyphen.

_____

_____

Apostrophes are used in grammatical contractions. They show that letters have been left out.

(e) In the text, add the missing apostrophes in 11 contractions.

(f) Write the 5 different contractions used in the text in full below.

❷ Spelling

(a) Underline 4 spelling mistakes in the text and write them correctly below.

_____

_____

❸ Grammar

(a) Indicate the tense of these verbs from the text by writing "past," "future," or "present" after each.

(i)   knows   _____

(ii) shook   _____

(iii) dropped   _____

(iv) am going to weed   _____

School Concert

Lesson Focus

Punctuation

- Hyphens
- Grammatical commas
- Periods
- Exclamation marks

Grammar

- Adverbs

Spelling

- Misspelled words
- Confused words: whole/hole
- Plurals ("s" and "es")

Vocabulary

- Enrichment – musical instruments

Teacher Information

A recount retells events as they happen, in time order. Recounts are written using verbs in the past tense.

Answers

Dear Diary,

Today was the big day**!** I felt so *nervous* about playing my guitar in front of the *whole* school. There were twenty**-**two of us from different *classes* waiting offstage to perform**,** all with *different* instruments. When my name was called**,** I <u>slowly</u> walked on**.** I had a heart**-**stopping moment *when* I almost dropped my *guitar*. But once I'd sat down and started playing, I felt much better. I made a few *mistakes,* but I managed to keep going, so I *hope* no one noticed! When I'd finished, the audience began to applaud <u>loudly</u>**.** It felt great**!** I haven't stopped *smiling* yet**.** I can't wait to play again.

| nervous |
| whole |
| classes |
| different |
| slowly |
| when |
| guitar |
| mistakes |
| hope |
| loudly |
| smiling |

1. Missing punctuation is in **bold type**.

2. (a) Adverbs are <u>underlined</u>.

     slowly, loudly

   (b) Teacher check

3. Spelling errors are in *italic type*.

   (a) classes, mistakes

   (b) nervous, whole, different, when, guitar, hope, smiling

4. (a) Teacher check. Answers may include: piano, harp, violin, viola, cello, double bass, banjo, mandolin, etc.

School Concert

Read the diary entry.

Dear Diary,

Today was the big day I felt so nervos about   _____

playing my guitar in front of the hole school.   _____

There were twentytwo of us from different clases   _____

waiting offstage to perform all with diferent instruments.   _____

When my name was called I slow walked on I had   _____

a heartstopping moment wen I almost dropped my   _____

gitar. But once I'd sat down and started playing, I felt   _____

much better. I made a few mistaks, but I managed to   _____

keep going, so I hop no one noticed! When I'd finished,   _____

the audience began to applaud loud It felt great I   _____

haven't stopped smilling yet I can't wait to play again.   _____

❶ Punctuation

(a) Find the 2 missing commas and 3 periods.

(b) Find the 2 missing hyphens and 2 exclamation marks.

❷ Grammar

Adverbs are words that describe verbs, telling "how," "when," or "why" something happens. They often end in "ly"; for example, "happily," "quickly."

(a) Write the 2 adverbs that are missing the "ly" ending in the space at the end of the line.

(b) Add adverbs to describe the verbs in these sentences. They do not have to end in "ly."

  (i) Her hands shook _____.

  (ii) The audience listened _____.

  (iii) Although I don't practice _____, I am improving.

❸ Spelling

(a) Two plural words from the text are spelled incorrectly. Write the correct spelling in the space at the end of the line.

(b) Write the 7 other misspelled words correctly in the space at the end of the line.

❹ Vocabulary

(a) List as many musical instruments with strings as you can. Use a dictionary to make sure your spelling is correct.

guitar,

Glow-Worm Grotto

Lesson Focus

Punctuation

- Capital letters for proper nouns
- Capital letters for sentence beginnings
- Periods
- Hyphens
- Exclamation marks

Grammar

- Adverbs
- Subject-verb agreement
- Prepositions

Spelling

- Confused words: quite/quiet
- Misspelled words

Teacher Information

A description describes the characteristics, components or functions of specific living or non-living things.

Answers

The glow-worm *grotto* in the Te Ana-au caves in the South Island of **N**ew **Z**ealand is well *worth* visiting. After you walk <u>carefully</u> into the caves, you are *asked* to get into a small boat to enter the grotto**.** **W**hen you get there, it is absolutely *quiet* and pitch black. The only light you can <u>see</u> is from the glow-worms, which <u>are</u> dotted above you. They look like tiny blue stars. It feels eerie to be <u>silently</u> gliding under them with no other *light* or sound**.** **Y**ou can't *even* see your own hand in front of your face**.** **B**y the time you <u>leave</u> the grotto, you feel disoriented—it is *difficult* to say which way is up or down**!**

grotto
worth
carefully
asked
quiet
see
are
silently
light
even
leave
difficult

Answers

1. (a) Missing punctuation is in **bold type**.

   (b) Answers should include two of the following: glow-worm, Te Ana-au, pitch-black

2. (a) Adverbs are <u>underlined</u>.

   carefully, silently

   (b) Verbs are <u>underlined in bold</u>.

   see (line 6), are (line 7), leave (line 11)

   (c) (i) into (ii) from (iii) under

   (iv) in (v) above (vi) to

3. (a) Spelling errors are in *italic type*.

   grotto, worth, asked, quiet, light, even, difficult

Glow-Worm Grotto

Read the description.

The glow-worm groto in the Te Ana-au caves in the

_____

South Island of new zealand is well werth visiting.

_____

After you walk **with care** into the caves, you are

_____

aksed to get into a small boat to enter the grotto

_____

when you get there, it is absolutely quite and

_____

pitch black. The only light you can sees is from the

_____

glow-worms, which is dotted above you. They look

_____

like tiny blue stars. It feels eerie to be **in silence** gliding

_____

under them with no other lite or sound you can't

_____

evin see your own hand in front of your face by the

_____

time you leaves the grotto, you feel disoriented—it is

_____

dificult to say which way is up or down

_____

❶ Punctuation

(a) Find the 5 missing capital letters, 3 periods and 1 exclamation mark.

A hyphen (-) is used in some compound words to connect smaller words together; for example, happy-go-lucky, self-pity.

(b) Write two hyphenated compound words used in this text.

❷ Grammar

Adverbs are words that describe verbs; for example, "happily," "slowly," "often."

(a) Look at the words in bold type in the text. Replace each group of words with one adverb with the same meaning and write it in the space at the end of the line.

In any sentence, the subject and the verb have to agree in person and in number; for example, "He **sees**" but "They **see**."

(b) Three verbs in the text do not agree with their subjects. Write the correct form of each verb in the space at the end of the line.

Prepositions are positional words placed before nouns and pronouns to indicate their relation to other words; for example, "caves **in** the South Island."

(c) Underline the prepositions in each sentence.

  (i) You can walk into the caves.

  (ii) The light is from the glow-worms.

  (iii) We were gliding under them.

  (iv) The grotto is in the caves.

  (v) The glow-worms are dotted above you.

  (vi) They enjoyed their visit to the caves.

❸ Spelling

(a) Write the correct spelling for the misspelled words in the space at the end of the line.

How Does a Microwave Oven Work?

Lesson Focus

Punctuation

- Capital letters for sentence beginnings
- Grammatical commas
- Commas in lists
- Parentheses
- Apostrophes in contractions

Grammar

- Verb tenses
- Adverbs

Spelling

- Confused words: threw/through, there/their
- Misspelled words

Vocabulary

- Antonyms

Teacher Information

An explanation seeks to explain how something works, is made, or how or why things happen.

Answers

A microwave oven cooks food from the inside *out*. Here**'**s how it *works*. **W**hen you press "start" on the oven**,** microwaves (short radio waves**)** are *produced*. These waves pass *through* any glass**,** paper or plastic containers you have put in the oven and <u>quickly</u> find *their* way into the food. **T**he microwaves then make the water and fat molecules in the food *vibrate***,** causing heat. This is what warms up your *favorite* hot drink or cooks your food**.** **I**t is *usually* much quicker than cooking with an *electric* or gas oven. This is because these ovens work by *heating* food <u>gradually</u> from the outside in.

out
works
produced
through
quickly
their
vibrate
favorite
usually
electric
heating
gradually

1. (a) Missing punctuation is in **bold type**.

2. (a) (i) cooked   (ii) worked   (iii) warmed   (iv) pressed

   (b) Adverbs are <u>underlined in bold</u>.

   quickly, gradually

3. Spelling errors are in *italic type*.

   out, works, produced, through, their, vibrate, favorite, usually, electric, heating

4. Possible answers.

   (i) slowly   (ii) lose   (iii) cooling

   (iv) mine, our   (v) suddenly

How Does a Microwave Oven Work?

Read the explanation.

A microwave oven cooks food from the inside owt.   _____

Heres how it werks. when you press "start" on the   _____

oven microwaves (short radio waves are prodused.   _____

These waves pass threw any glass paper or plastic   _____

containers you have put in the oven and quick find   _____

there way into the food. the microwaves then make   _____

the water and fat molecules in the food vibbrate   _____

causing heat. This is what warms up your favorrite   _____

hot drink or cooks your food. it is usally much   _____

quicker than cooking with an electrick or gas oven.   _____

This is because these ovens work by heeting food   _____

gradual from the outside in.   _____

❶ *Punctuation*

(a) Find 3 missing capital letters, 1 comma in a list, 2 grammatical commas, 1 apostrophe for a contraction and 1 parenthesis for additional information.

❷ *Grammar*

This explanation uses verbs in the present tense. Present tense verbs often end in "s."

(a) Write these present tense verbs ending in "s" from the text in the past tense.

   (i)   cooks _____

   (ii) works _____

   (iii) warms _____

   (iv) press _____

Adverbs are words that describe verbs. They often end in "ly"; for example, "happily," "slowly."

(b) Two adverbs from the text are missing the "ly" ending. Write them correctly in the space at the end of the line.

❸ *Spelling*

(a) Write the correct spelling of 10 misspelled words in the space at the end of the line.

❹ *Vocabulary*

Antonyms are words with opposite meanings; for example, inside – outside.

(a) Write an antonym for each of these.

   (i)   quickly _____

   (ii) find _____

   (iii) heating _____

   (iv) your _____

   (v) gradually _____

Roald Dahl

Lesson Focus

Punctuation

- Capital letters for proper nouns
- Colons in offset lists
- Hyphens
- Parentheses

Spelling

- Misspelled words
- Confused words: son/sun

Grammar

- Subject-verb agreement

Vocabulary

- Shortened forms

Teacher Information

A recount retells events as they happened, in time order. Recounts are usually written using verbs in the past tense.

Answers

> Roald Dahl **(**1916 – 1990**)**
>
> Roald Dahl was a well-loved children's *author*. He <u>was</u> born in **W**ales in 1916, the *son* of **N**orwegian *parents*. After he finished his schooling in **E**ngland, he began *work* for the Shell Oil Company and <u>was</u> posted to **A**frica a few years later. *When* World War II broke out, he enlisted as a fighter pilot in the <u>RAF</u>. In 1942, he *moved* to the <u>USA</u> and began to *write* stories.
>
> **D**ahl's children's books include**:**
>
> - **C**harlie and the *Chocolate* Factory,
> - **T**he <u>BFG</u>, and
> - **J**ames and the Giant Peach.

1. (a) Missing punctuation is in **bold type**.

   (c) Teacher check

2. (a) Verbs are <u>underlined</u>.

   "He was" (line 1), "and was" (line 3)

3. (a) Spelling errors are in *italic type*.

   author, son, parents, work, When, moved, write, chocolate

4. (a) Shortened forms (in this case, initialisms) are <u>underlined in bold</u>.

   RAF – Royal Air Force

   USA – United States of America

   BFG – Big Friendly Giant

   (b) (i) prof.   (ii) AIDS   (iii) sch.   (iv) scuba

Roald Dahl

Read the biography.

Roald Dahl 1916 – 1990

Roald Dahl was a well-loved children's aufor. He were born in wales in 1916, the sun of norwegian parrents. After he finished his schooling in england, he began werk for the Shell Oil Company and were posted to africa a few years later. Wen World War II broke out, he enlisted as a fighter pilot in the RAF. In 1942, he mooved to the USA and began to rite stories.

dahl's children's books include

• charlie and the choclate factory,

• the BFG, and

• james and the giant peach.

❶ *Punctuation*

(a) Add parentheses to the title.

(b) Write 10 missing capital letters and the colon missing from the offset list.

A hyphen (-) is used in some compound words to connect smaller words together; for example, "happy-go-lucky," "self-pity."

(c) The word "well-loved" in this text uses a hyphen. Use a dictionary to find three other words beginning with "well" that also use a hyphen.

❷ *Grammar*

*In any sentence, the subject and the verb have to agree in person and in number; for example, "He **sees**" but "They **see**."*

(a) Two verbs in the text do not agree with their subjects. Write the correct form of each verb above the text.

❸ *Spelling*

(a) Write the correct spelling of the 8 words which are misspelled.

_____

_____

_____

_____

❹ *Vocabulary*

(a) Circle 3 shortened forms used in the text. Write what each stands for.

(i) _____

(ii) _____

(iii) _____

(b) Write the shortened form for:

(i) professor _____

(ii) acquired immune deficiency syndrome _____

(iii) school _____

(iv) self-contained underwater breathing apparatus _____

© World Teachers Press® ~ www.worldteacherspress.com

How Chewing Gum Is Made

Lesson Focus

Punctuation

- Capital letters for sentence beginnings
- Periods
- Grammatical commas
- Colons in offset lists

Grammar

- Subject-verb agreement
- Prepositions

Spelling

- Confused words: witch/which, mane/main
- Misspelled words
- Plurals ("s" and "es")

Teacher Information

An explanation outlines how something works, is made or how or why things happen.

Answers

Chewing gum is made with three basic ingredients: gum base, sweeteners and flavorings.
The *main* ingredient of chewing gum is the gum base, *which* is like rubber. It makes the gum chewy and also gives it a smooth *texture*. When chewing gum <u>was</u> first produced, gum base was made from tree sap, but now *artificial* gum bases are used. As the gum base gets warm in your mouth, it *softens* and the flavor of the gum is *released*. Sweeteners and flavorings <u>are</u> added to the gum base. The most *common* sweeteners added to chewing gum are sugar and corn *syrup*. The most popular flavorings used in chewing gum are *peppermint* and spearmint.

main	
which	
texture	
was	
artifical	
softens	
released	
are	
common	
syrup	
peppermint	

1. (a) Missing punctuation is in **bold type**.

2. (a) Verbs are <u>underlined</u>.

   were – was (line 8), is – are (line 12)

   (b) (i) hate   (ii) buy   (iii) take   (iv) hides

   (c) with, of, from, in (x2)

   (d) Teacher check

3. (a) Spelling errors are in *italic type*.

   main, which, texture, artificial, softens, released, common, syrup, peppermint

How Chewing Gum Is Made

Read the explanation.

Chewing gum is made **with** three basic ingredients gum base, sweeteners, and flavorings.

The mane ingredient **of** chewing gum is the gum _____

base witch is like rubber it makes the gum chewy _____

and also gives it a smooth tecksture. When chewing _____

gum were first produced gum base was made **from** tree _____

sap, but now artificiall gum bases are used as the _____

gum base gets warm **in** your mouth it soffens and _____

the flavor of the gum is releesed sweeteners and _____

flavorings is added to the gum base. The most _____

commonn sweeteners added to chewing gum are _____

sugar and corn sirup the most popular flavorings _____

used **in** chewing gum are pepermint and spearmint. _____

❶ Punctuation

(a) Write the 4 missing capital letters, 4 periods, 3 commas and the colon missing from the offset list.

❷ Grammar

*In any sentence, the subject and the verb have to agree in person and in number; for example, "He **chews**" but "They **chew**."*

(a) Two verbs in the text do not agree with their subjects. Write the correct form of each verb in the space at the end of each line where it is found.

(b) Circle the correct verbs.

(i) Mom and Dad hate/hates chewing gum.

(ii) We buy/buys it regularly.

(iii) I takes/take it to chew after school.

(iv) My sister hide/hides it.

Prepositions are positional words placed before nouns and pronouns to indicate their relation to other words; for example, "under," "for," "by."

(c) Find the 4 different prepositions in bold type in the text and write them below.

(d) Write 2 sentences, using one of these prepositions in each.

_____

_____

_____

_____

_____

❸ Spelling

(a) Write the misspelled words correctly in the space at the end of the line.

Flying Carpet

Lesson Focus

Punctuation

- Periods
- Grammatical commas
- Question marks
- Apostrophes for grammatical contractions
- Quotation marks for direct speech

Grammar

- Adverbs

Spelling

- Misspelled words
- Plurals ("s" and "es")

Teacher Information

Narratives tell a story in a sequence of events.

Answers

> "Antique shops are so boring**,**" sighed Alex**.** "When do you think Mom will be finished**?**" He glanced <u>swiftly</u> over his *shoulder*. She was inspecting some dusty glasses.
>
> **"**Soon, I hope**,**" said Shane, *scuffing* his shoes on the floor. "Then …" He *stopped* suddenly and gasped**.**
>
> "What's *wrong***?**" asked Alex.
>
> **"**That rug … it**'**s hovering!**"**
>
> "What are you talking about**?**" Alex looked *where* Shane was pointing**.** Next to a *stack* of boxes, a ratty blue rug he hadn't *noticed* before was *floating* a few inches above the *floorboards***.**
>
> "It must be a trick**,**" said Shane. He <u>carefully</u> placed one foot on the rug**.** It rose slightly and *began* flapping <u>quickly</u>.
>
> "I think it wants to go somewhere," *whispered* Alex. "I don**'**t think it**'**s a trick**,** Shane. This must be a real flying carpet**.**"

1. Missing punctuation is in **bold type**.
2. (a) Adverbs are <u>underlined</u>.
   swiftly, carefully, quickly
3. (a) Spelling errors are in *italic type*.
   shoulder, scuffing, stopped, wrong, where, stack, noticed, floating, floorboards, began, whispered
   (b) glasses, boxes, Teacher check

Flying Carpet

Read the diary narrative.

"Antique shops are so boring" sighed Alex "When do you think Mom will be finished" He glanced swift over his sholder. She was inspecting some dusty glasses.

Soon, I hope said Shane, scufing his shoes on the floor. "Then ..." He stoped suddenly and gasped

"What's rong" asked Alex.

That rug ... its hovering!

"What are you talking about" Alex looked wher Shane was pointing Next to a stak of boxes, a ratty blue rug he hadn't notised before was flowting a few inches above the florboards.

"It must be a trick" said Shane. He carefull placed one foot on the rug It rose slightly and beggan flapping quick.

"I think it wants to go somewhere," wispered Alex. "I dont think its a trick Shane. This must be a real flying carpet"

❶ *Punctuation*

(a) Write the 4 missing commas, 5 periods, 3 question marks and 3 apostrophes.

The actual words spoken by a person are called direct speech. This begins and ends with quotation marks.

(b) Write in the 2 sets of quotation marks missing from the direct speech in the text.

❷ *Grammar*

Adverbs are words that describe verbs. They often end in "ly"; for example, "happily," "slowly."

(a) Three adverbs from the text are missing the "ly" ending. Write them correctly below.

_____

_____

_____

❸ *Spelling*

(a) Write the correct spelling of the 11 misspelled words.

(b) Write two plural words from the text that end in "es." Add three more plurals of your own that end in "es."

_____

_____

_____

Letter to the Editor

Lesson Focus

Punctuation

- Apostrophes to show possession
- Capital letters for proper nouns
- Question marks
- Quotation marks for direct speech

Grammar

- Subject-verb agreement
- Pronouns

Spelling

- Confused words: not/knot
- Misspelled words

Teacher Information

An exposition can analyze, interpret and evaluate. Its purpose is to persuade by presenting one side of an argument.

Answers

March 12, 2006

Dear Sir:

I am concerned about the **L**illydale **C**ouncil**'**s *proposal* to *chop* down 20 trees in **B**aker **P**ark to make way for an outdoor cinema. Baker Park**'**s trees <u>are</u> precious. Some of <u>them</u> are more than 50 years old and they <u>provide</u> many animals and birds with a home.

proposal
chop
are
them
provide

Councillor **C**andace **Q**uigley said *yesterday,* "Baker Park is the only possible site for the *cinema.***"** <u>She</u> is not correct. There are three other parks in the local area, all of which <u>have</u> plenty of treeless space for the cinema. Why *not* use one of these**?**

yesterday
cinema
She
have
not

An outdoor cinema would be a *wonderful* addition to our community**'**s *facilities*, but not at the cost of our environment. What <u>are</u> other people**'**s opinions**?**

wonderful
facilities
are

Yours sincerely,

Charlotte **J**ohnson

Answers

1. (a) Missing punctuation is in **bold type**.

   (b) Teacher check

2. (a) Verbs are <u>underlined</u>.

      are, provide, have, are

   (b) Pronouns are <u>**underlined in bold**</u>.

      them (it), She (Her)

3. (a) Spelling errors are in *italic type*.

      proposal, chop, yesterday, cinema, not, wonderful, facilities

Letter to the Editor

Read the exposition in the form of a letter.

March 12, 2006

Dear Sir:

I am concerned about the lillydale councils proposel   _____

to chopp down 20 trees in baker park to make way for   _____

an outdoor cinema. Baker Parks trees is precious.   _____

Some of it are more than 50 years old and they   _____

provides many animals and birds with a home.   _____

Councillor candace quigley said yestaday, "Baker Park   _____

is the only possible site for the sinema.   _____

Her is not correct. There are three other parks in the local   _____

area, all of which has plenty of treeless space for the   _____

cinema. Why knot use one of these   _____

An outdoor cinema would be a wonderfull addition to   _____

our communitys fasilities, but not at the cost of our   _____

environment. What is other peoples opinions   _____

Yours sincerely,

Charlotte johnson

❶ Punctuation

(a) Add 4 missing apostrophes to show possession, 7 capital letters for proper nouns, 2 question marks and the missing quotation mark.

(b) Write today's date using the same form and punctuation as the letter.

❷ Grammar

*In any sentence, the subject and the verb have to agree in person and in number. For example, "He **writes**" but "They **write**."*

(a) Four verbs in the text do not agree with their subjects. Write the correct form of each verb in the space at the end of the line.

Pronouns are words that replace nouns; e.g. "I," "he," "she," "him," "it."

(b) Circle the 2 incorrect pronouns used in the text. Write the correct pronouns in the space at the end of each line.

❸ Spelling

(a) Write the correct spelling for each of the 7 misspelled words in the space at the end of the line.

Book Review

Lesson Focus

Punctuation

- Apostrophes to show possession
- Capital letters for titles
- Capital letters for proper nouns
- Hyphens

Grammar

- Conjunctions
- Verb tenses

Spelling

- Confused words: by/bye, would/wood, real/reel, to/too/two, for/four
- Misspelled words
- Plurals ("es")

Teacher Information

A report is usually written in the present tense and gives facts clearly, without unnecessary information or opinions.

Answers

Disastrous! *by* John **C**han is an older children's book that <u>describes</u> all sorts of natural and human‑created disasters, from shipwrecks *to* <u>volcanoes</u>. Any child with an *interest* in science and technology *would* enjoy this book.

The text is easy to read and <u>contains</u> lists of little‑known facts and quotes from *real* <u>eyewitnesses</u>. The photographs and illustrations are *bright* and interesting, but sometimes they are a bit *too* violent *for* the target age group of the book. Chan's book also <u>leaves</u> out some of the more well‑known disasters, like the *sinking* of the **T**itanic and the **B**lack Death. But the disasters he <u>includes</u> have been well‑researched and make *fascinating* reading.

by
describes
to
interest
would
contains
real
bright
too
for
leaves
sinking
includes
fascinating

1. (a) Missing punctuation is in **bold type**.

   Hyphenated words are: human-created, little-known, well-known, well-researched

2. (a) Answers should include two of the following: and, but, that

   (b) Verbs are <u>underlined</u>.

   describes, contains, leaves, includes

3. (a) Spelling errors are in *italic type*.

   by, to, interest, would, real, bright, too, for, sinking, fascinating

   (b) Plural words are <u>**underlined in bold**</u>.

   volcanoes, eyewitnesses, Teacher check

Book Review

Read the book review.

disastrous! bye John chan is an older childrens

book that will describe all sorts of natural and

human-created disasters, from shipwrecks too

volcanoes. Any child with an intrest in science

and technology wood enjoy this book.

The text is easy to read and will contain lists of

little-known facts and quotes from reel eyewitnesses.

The photographs and illustrations are brite and

interesting but sometimes they are a bit two

violent four the target age group of the book. Chans

book also will leave out some of the more well-known

disasters, like the sincking of the titanic and the black

Death. But the disasters he will include have been

well-researched and make facinating reading.

❶ Punctuation

(a) Add 2 missing apostrophes for possession and 4 missing capital letters. Circle the 4 hyphenated words.

❷ Grammar

Conjunctions are words that join single words or groups of words to make a sentence longer; for example, "and," "or," "because."

(a) Write two conjunctions used in the text.

(b) Four of the verbs in this text are incorrect because they are written in the future tense (e.g. "He will write"). Write the correct present tense of each of these verbs in the space at the end of the line.

❸ Spelling

(a) Write the 10 misspelled words correctly in the space at the end of the line.

To make the plural of some nouns, "es" is added. This includes most singular words that end in "s," "ss," "sh," "o," "ch," "x" and "z."

(b) Write two plural nouns from the text that end in "es." Write two more plural nouns of your own that end in "es."

Aquatic Biomes

Lesson Focus

Punctuation

- Capital letters for sentence beginnings
- Periods
- Grammatical commas
- Commas for lists

Grammar

- Subject-verb agreement

Spelling

- Confused words: were/where, seas/sees, witch/which, dew/due, sun/son, sum/some, there/their

Writing

- Paragraphs

Teacher Information

An explanation seeks to explain what something is, how it functions, or is made.

Answers

A biome _is_ a large community of animals and plants living in a particular environment. The two major types of biomes are terrestrial and aquatic. Aquatic biomes are either freshwater or saltwater.

Freshwater biomes include lakes**,** rivers and wetlands. The shoreline of a lake is shallow and warm**,** inhabited by insects and amphibians. In the center**,** the water is deeper and colder and _is_ home to fish and crustaceans. Rivers are much colder still**,** supporting fish**,** floating weeds**,** algae and fungi. The greatest variety of animal and plant life can be found in wetlands**,** _where_ the waters are still and the atmosphere humid.

Saltwater biomes include all the _seas_ and oceans**.** **T**hey are the largest and most diverse of all biomes**.** **T**hey have many zones _which_ vary in temperature _due_ to the amount of sunlight they _receive_. **T**he open ocean is home to many fish, marine mammals, plankton and seaweed**.** **W**here the _sun_ cannot penetrate, in the deepest depths of the oceans, it is pitch black, very cold and the pressure _is_ enormous**.** **I**n spite of such inhospitable conditions, _some_ animals _have_ adapted to living _there_**.**

1. (a) Missing punctuation is in **bold type**.

2. (a) Verbs are underlined.

   (i) are – a biome ✗   (ii) include – biomes ✓

   (iii) is – the water ✓   (iv) receives – the zones ✗

   (v) is – the pressure ✓   (vi) has – animals ✗

3. (a) Spelling errors are in _italic type_.

   where, seas, which, due, sun, some, there

4. (a) Answers will vary but should approximate the following:

   Paragraph 2 "What are freshwater biomes like?"

   Paragraph 3 "What are saltwater biomes like?"

Aquatic Biomes

Read the explanation.

A biome **are** a large community of animals and plants living in a particular environment. The two major types of biomes are terrestrial and aquatic. Aquatic biomes are either freshwater or saltwater.

Freshwater biomes **include** lakes rivers and wetlands. The shoreline of a lake is shallow and warm inhabited by insects and amphibians. In the center the water is deeper and colder and **is** home to fish and crustaceans. Rivers are much colder still supporting fish floating weeds algae and fungi. The greatest variety of animal and plant life can be found in wetlands (were/where) the waters are still and the atmosphere humid.

saltwater biomes include all the (seas/sees) and oceans they are the largest and most diverse of all biomes they have many zones (witch/which) vary in temperature (dew/due) to the amount of sunlight they **receives** the open ocean is home to many fish, marine mammals, plankton and seaweed where the (sun/son) cannot penetrate, in the deepest depths of the oceans, it is pitch black, very cold and the pressure **is** enormous in spite of such inhospitable conditions, (sum/some) animals **has** adapted to living (there/their)

❶ Punctuation

(a) Paragraph 3 contains 6 sentences. Add the missing capital letters and periods.

(b) Paragraph 2 requires 7 commas. Write them in.

❷ Grammar

The subject and verb must always be in agreement.

(a) Circle the subject to which the verbs in bold print in the text relate. Write a tick (✓) or a cross (✗) in the box to show if they are in agreement.

(i) are ☐   (ii) include ☐

(iii) is ☐   (iv) receives ☐

(v) is ☐   (vi) has ☐

❸ Spelling

(a) Circle the correct spelling where a choice of words is given.

❹ Writing

(a) The text is divided into paragraphs. Each paragraph describes a new thought or idea. The first paragraph answers the question "What is an aquatic biome?" Write a question that is answered by each of the last two paragraphs.

Paragraph 2

_____

_____

_____

Paragraph 3

_____

_____

_____

_____

Treating a Nosebleed

Lesson Focus

Punctuation

- Grammatical commas
- Periods
- Apostrophes in grammatical contractions

Grammar

- Imperative verbs
- Adverbs

Spelling

- Confused words: hear/here, through/threw, four/for
- Misspelled words

Vocabulary

- Compound words

Teacher Information

A procedure outlines how something is done. It gives a list of materials or requirements and instructions using imperative (command) verbs.

Answers

If you get a <u>nosebleed</u>**,** *here* is what you *should* do.

- <u>Breathe</u> *through* your mouth.
- <u>Sit</u> down and <u>lean forward</u> *slightly*.
- <u>Apply</u> *pressure* to your nostrils with your finger and *thumb***.**
- <u>Ask</u> <u>someone</u> to gently place wet *towels* on your neck and your <u>forehead</u>**.**
- If the bleeding hasn**'**t stopped *after* 10 minutes**,** firmly <u>press</u> your nostrils again *for* another 10 minutes**.** If it doesn**'**t stop after this**,** <u>go</u> to the *doctor*.

here
should
through
slightly
pressure
thumb
gently
towels
after
firmly
for
doctor

1. (a) Missing punctuation is in **bold type**.

2. (a) Command verbs are <u>underlined</u>. Possible answers include:

   Breathe, Sit, lean, Apply, Ask, press, go

   (b) slightly, gently, firmly

3. Spelling errors are in *italic type*.

   (a) here, through, for

   (b) should, pressure, thumb, towels, after, doctor

4. (a) Compound words are <u>underlined in bold</u>.

   nosebleed, forward, someone, forehead

   (b) Teacher check. Possible answers include: mouthguard, mouthpiece, mouth-to-mouth, mouthwash, mouth-watering, loudmouth, badmouth

Treating a Nosebleed

Read the procedure.

If you get a nosebleed (hear/here) is what you

shoud do.

_____

_____

• Breathe (through/threw) your mouth.

_____

• Sit down and lean forward a **slight amount**.

_____

• Apply presure to your nostrils with your

finger and thum

_____

_____

• Ask someone to **with gentlenesss** place wet

towls on your neck and your forehead

_____

_____

• If the bleeding hasnt stopped afta 10

minutes **with firmness** press your nostrils again

(four/for) another 10 minutes If it doesnt stop after

this go to the docter.

_____

_____

_____

_____

❶ Punctuation

(a) Add 3 missing commas, 2 apostrophes for grammatical contractions and 3 periods.

❷ Grammar

Command verbs are used in procedures, often at the beginning of sentences. They tell us what to do; for example, "**Paint** the rose pink," "**Stand** up."

(a) Write 4 command verbs from the text.

Adverbs are words that describe verbs. They often end in "ly"; for example, "happily," "slowly."

(b) Look at the words in bold type in the text. Replace each group of words with one adverb with the same meaning. Write it in the space at the end of the line.

❸ Spelling

(a) Choose the correct spelling from each pair of words in brackets. Write your choice in the space at the end of the line.

(b) Write the correct spelling of the 6 misspelled words in the space at the end of the line.

❹ Vocabulary

Compound words are made up of two smaller words; for example, "rainbow."

(a) Circle 2 compound words found in this text.

(b) Write 3 compound words containing the word "mouth."

How Does Velcro® Work?

Lesson Focus

Punctuation

- Capital letters for sentence beginnings
- Grammatical commas
- Commas in lists
- Apostrophes to show possession
- Exclamation marks

Grammar

- Subject-verb agreement
- Adjectives

Spelling

- Misspelled words

Vocabulary

- Antonyms
- Synonyms

Teacher Information

An explanation seeks to explain how things work or how or why things happen.

Answers

Velcro <u>is</u> a <u>handy</u> fastener you will have seen on shoes**,** clothes and other *everyday* objects. **Y**ou <u>need</u> <u>two</u> <u>different</u> strips of velcro to make it work. One of the strips <u>has</u> <u>tiny</u> <u>nylon</u> or <u>polyester</u> hooks all over it. The other strip is *covered* in nylon loops, although it <u>feels</u> <u>furry</u> to touch. **W**hen the <u>two</u> strips are pressed together**,** the hooks <u>grab</u> the loops so the strips are held firmly. **T**he *clever* thing about velcro <u>is</u> that it can be pulled apart and rejoined—thousands of times over. **T**he *inventor* of velcro got the idea from trying to pull *prickles* out of his dog**'**s *fur***!**

is
everyday
need
has
covered
feels
grab
clever
is
inventor
prickles
fur

1. (a) Missing punctuation is in **bold type**.

2. (a) Verbs are <u>underlined</u>.

    Velcro <u>is</u>, you <u>need</u>, one of the strips <u>has</u>, it <u>feels</u>, hooks <u>grab</u>, velcro <u>is</u>

    (b) (i) Adjectives are <u>underlined in bold</u>.

    Answers should include three of the following: handy, everyday, different, tiny, nylon, polyester, furry, two, clever

    (ii) Teacher check

3. (a) Spelling errors are in *italic type*.

    everyday, covered, clever, inventor, prickles, fur

4. (a) Teacher check. Possible answers include:

    (i) same, similar (ii) together (iii) uncovered

    (iv) pull

    (b) (i) snatch (ii) detach, divide (iii) hide, conceal

    (iv) labor, toil

How Does Velcro® Work?

Read the explanation.

Velcro are a handy fastener you will have seen _____

on shoes clothes and other everday objects. you _____

needs two different strips of velcro to make it work. _____

One of the strips have tiny nylon or polyester hooks all _____

over it. The other strip is coverred in nylon loops, _____

although it feel furry to touch. when the two strips are _____

pressed together the hooks grabs the loops so _____

the strips are held firmly. the clevver thing _____

about velcro are that it can be pulled apart and _____

rejoined thousands of times over. the inventer _____

of velcro got the idea from trying to pull prikles _____

out of his dogs furr _____

❶ Punctuation

(a) Add the 4 missing capital letters, 2 commas, 1 apostrophe to show possession and 1 exclamation mark.

❷ Grammar

*In any sentence, the subject and the verb have to agree in person and in number; for example, "He **pulls**" but "They **pull**."*

(a) Six verbs in the text do not agree with their subjects. Write the correct form of each verb in the space at the end of the line.

*Adjectives are words that describe nouns; for example, **red** car, **juicy** apple.*

(b) (i) Circle 3 adjectives in the text.

(ii) List at least 3 adjectives you can think of that describe velcro.

❸ Spelling

(a) Write the correct spelling of 6 misspelled words in the space at the end of each line.

❹ Vocabulary

Antonyms are words with opposite meanings.

(a) Write an antonym for each.

(i)   different _____

(ii) apart _____

(iii) covered _____

(iv) press _____

Synonyms are words with similar meanings.

(b) Write a synonym for each verb.

(i)   grab _____

(ii) separate _____

(iii) cover _____

(iv) work _____

Trees Cross Railway Line

Lesson Focus

Punctuation

- Capital letters for sentence beginnings
- Periods

Spelling

- Confused words: two/too/to, their/there, brought/bought, witch/which, threw/through
- Misspelled words

Grammar

- Prepositions

Vocabulary

- Enrichment

Teacher Information

A recount retells events as they happened, in time order. Recounts are usually written using verbs in the past tense.

Answers

People watched in disbelief yesterday as *two* trees which had been major landmarks in *their* small town came crashing down on to the railway line**.**

Just after 3 p.m., an ear-splitting thunderclap sounded and lightning struck the larger tree**. A** huge fissure appeared in the body of the tree and it collapsed**. A**s it fell, it *brought* down the second tree, already *weakened* by the day's barrage of nature's anger**. I**t is a miracle that no one was injured**. T**he debris from both trees was scattered across the platforms and the town *square***.**

As if satisfied with its work, nature commanded the wind and rain to *calm*, and the thunder and lightning to cease**. E**ven the sun, *which* had been hiding all afternoon behind thick storm clouds, was tempted to peep *through* and shed more *light* on the devastation**.**

Answers

1. (a) Missing punctuation is in **bold type**.

2. (a) (i) in (ii) with (iii) across

   (iv) of (v) by (vi) behind

   (b) Teacher check

3. Spelling errors are in italic type.

   (a) two, their, brought, which, through

   (b) weakened, square, calm, light

4. (a) (i) command (ii) barrage (iii) debris

   (iv) collapse (v) fissure

Trees Cross Railway Line

Read this recount.

people watched in disbelief yesterday as (two/too/to) trees which had been major landmarks in (their/there) small town came crashing down on to the railway line

just after 3 p.m., an ear-splitting thunderclap sounded and lightning struck the larger tree a huge fissure appeared in the body of the tree and it collapsed as it fell, it (brought/bought) down the second tree, already weekened by the day's barrage of nature's anger it is a miracle that no-one was injured the debris from both trees was scattered across the platforms and the town sqare

as if satisfied with its work, nature commanded the wind and rain to carm, and the thunder and lightning to cease even the sun, (witch/which) had been hiding all afternoon behind thick storm clouds, was tempted to peep (threw/through) and shed more lite on the devastation

1 Punctuation
(a) Mark in the 8 capital letters and 8 periods.

2 Grammar
*Prepositions are positional words placed before nouns and pronouns to indicate their relation to other words; for example, "Put it **on** the table," "The dog is **under** the house."*

(a) Write in the missing prepositions from the text.

(i) landmarks _____ their town

(ii) satisfied _____ its work

(iii) scattered _____ the platforms

(iv) the body _____ the tree

(v) weakened _____ the day's barrage

(vi) hiding all afternoon _____ clouds

3 Spelling
(a) Circle the correct word in each bracket.

(b) Write the correct spelling of the 4 misspelled words.

4 Vocabulary
(a) Find a word from the text to match each definition.

(i) to order or direct

_____

(ii) an overwhelming attack

_____

(iii) rubbish left when something is destroyed

_____

(iv) to fall apart suddenly

_____

(v) a crack; a split

_____

Said the Teacup to the Saucer

Lesson Focus

Punctuation

- Capital letters for sentence beginnings
- Question marks
- Exclamation marks
- Quotation marks for direct speech

Spelling

- Misspelled words

Grammar

- Verbs
- Adverbs
- Nouns
- Adjectives

Vocabulary

- Synonyms

Teacher Information

A narrative tells a story involving fictional characters in a sequence of events.

Answers

> **"Y**ou're not important**!"** *laughed* the teacup to the saucer. **"I**'m the one who holds the drink that quenches the thirst**!"**
>
> **"M**aybe,**"** argued the saucer, **"**but I protect the *table* from marks and spills. **T**hat makes me very important**!"**
>
> **"I**'m such a *beautiful* shape,**"** continued the cup proudly, **"**for hands to warm themselves on a cold, winter night.**"**
>
> **"M**aybe,**"** *answered* the saucer wearily, **"**but who do the hands hold *when* you are too hot**?"**
>
> **"I** hold the drink**!"** stated the cup firmly. **"W**ithout me, there is no need for you**!"**
>
> **"M**aybe,**"** agreed the saucer with a smile, **"**but I hold you and the spoon and the *cookie*. **I**s there really no need for me**?"**
>
> **W**hat do you think**?**

1. (a) Missing punctuation is in **bold type**.
2. (a) Spelling errors are in *italic type*.

    laughed, table, beautiful, answered, when, cookie

3. (a) Teacher check
4. (a) laughed, argued, continued, answered, stated, agreed

    (b) Teacher check

Said the Teacup to the Saucer

Read the narrative.

you're not important larfed the teacup to the saucer. i'm the one who holds the drink that quenches the thirst

maybe, argued the saucer, but I protect the tabel from marks and spills. that makes me very important

i'm such a beatiful shape, continued the cup proudly, for hands to warm themselves on a cold, winter night

maybe, ansered the saucer wearily, but who do the hands hold wen you are too hot

i hold the drink stated the cup firmly. without me, there is no need for you

maybe, agreed the saucer with a smile, but I hold you and the spoon and the cooky. is there really no need for me

what do you think

➊ Punctuation

(a) Write in the 11 capital letters, 3 question marks and 5 exclamation marks.

Speech marks are put at the beginning and end of what is said by each person in a conversation.

(b) Add speech marks to the text.

➋ Spelling

(a) Underline the 6 misspelled words in the text and write them correctly below.

_____

_____

_____

➌ Grammar

(a) From the text, find:

(i) 3 verbs _____

_____

(ii) 3 adverbs _____

_____

(iii) 3 nouns _____

_____

(iv) 3 adjectives _____

_____

➍ Vocabulary

Synonyms are words with similar meanings.

(a) List all the words which are synonyms for the word "said."

(b) Write 3 synonyms for each of these words.

(i) went _____

_____

(ii) saw _____

_____

The Frilled Lizard

Lesson Focus

Punctuation

- Capital letters for sentence beginnings
- Capital letters for proper nouns
- Periods
- Grammatical commas

Grammar

- Pronouns – possessive
- Adjectives
- Nouns

Spelling

- Misspelled words

Teacher Information

A report is usually written in the present tense and gives facts clearly without unnecessary information or opinions.

Answers

The frilled lizard is famous for <u>its</u> ferocious *appearance*. **I**t is spectacular to watch as it raises the frills that *surround* <u>its</u> neck. **T**hese famous frills are *normally* folded away**.**

When the frilled lizard is *surprised* or frightened**,** it raises <u>its</u> frills in an *aggressive* display to scare off predators. **A**s the frills are *raised***,** the lizard also opens <u>its</u> mouth very wide and *emits* a hissing sound**,** adding to the threatening and dramatic *display***.**

The frilled lizard**,** which grows up to one *meter* long**,** is found in the northern parts of **A**ustralia and *drier* regions of **N**ew **G**uinea. It is *classed* as an "arboreal" animal because it is capable of *climbing* trees, from where it can spot <u>its</u> food, which is mainly *grasshoppers* and other small insects**.**

appearance
surround
normally
surprised
aggressive
raised
emits
display
meter
drier
classed
climbing
grasshoppers

1. Missing punctuation is in **bold type**.

2. (a) (i) yours   (ii) his   (iii) hers

      (iv) its   (v) ours   (vi) theirs

   (b) The word "its" has been <u>underlined</u>.

   (c) (i) aggressive   (ii) dramatic   (iii) spectacular

      (iv) threatening   (v) ferocious   (vi) arboreal

3. (a) Spelling errors are in *italic type*.

      appearance, surround, normally, surprised, aggressive, raised, emits, display, meter, drier, classed, climbing, grasshoppers

The Frilled Lizard

Read this report.

the frilled lizard is famous for its ferocious apearance it is   _____

spectacular to watch as it raises the frills that suround its   _____

neck these famous frills are normaly folded away   _____

when the frilled lizard is suprised or frightened it raises its   _____

frills in an agresive display to scare off predators as the   _____

frills are razed the lizard also opens its mouth very wide   _____

and emmitts a hissing sound adding to the threatening   _____

and dramatic dissplay   _____

the frilled lizard which grows up to one metre long is   _____

found in the northern parts of australia and dryer regions   _____

of new guinea it is clased as an "arboreal" animal because   _____

it is capable of climming trees, from where it can spot its food,   _____

which is mainly grashopers and other small insects   _____

❶ Punctuation

(a) Find the 10 missing capital letters, 7 periods and 5 commas.

❷ Grammar

While apostrophes are normally used to show possession, there are some words which mean "belonging to" that may cause confusion. There is no need to use an apostrophe in these words; for example, "his," "theirs."

(a) Write the possessive pronouns for:

(i) belonging to you   _____

(ii) belonging to him   _____

(iii) belonging to her   _____

(iv) belonging to it   _____

(v) belonging to us   _____

(vi) belonging to them   _____

(b) Which **possessive pronoun** has been used 5 times in the text?

_____

(c) Write an adjective from the text to match each noun below.

	noun	adjective
(i)	aggression	
(ii)	drama	
(iii)	spectacle	
(iv)	threat	
(v)	ferocity	
(vi)	arbor	

❸ Spelling

(a) There is a spelling mistake in each line of the text. Underline the error and write the correction in the space at the end of the line.

Missing Person

Lesson Focus

Punctuation

- Capital letters for proper nouns
- Colons in offset lists

Grammar

- Adjectives

Spelling

- Confused words: fore/for, blue/blew, by/buy, too/to, scene/seen
- Misspelled words

Vocabulary

- Shortened forms

Writing

- Double negatives

Teacher Information

A description describes the characteristics, components, or functions of living or nonliving things.

Answers

Police are concerned *for* the safety of VANESSA	for
HOYLE. **V**anessa was last seen two <u>weeks</u> ago near her	weeks
home in **B**lakeville, <u>Queensland</u>.	Queensland
Vanessa**:**	: (colon)
• is 20 <u>years</u> old	years
• is 172 <u>centimeters</u> tall and has a slim build	centimeters
• has *olive* skin, short black hair and brown eyes	olive
• speaks with an **A**merican *accent*	accent
• was wearing *blue* jeans and a white T-shirt	blue
with a *picture* of a cat on it	picture
at the time of her *disappearance*	disappearance
• may stop at a pharmacy to *buy* the medicine	buy
she needs *to* treat her asthma	to
• <u>didn't tell anyone</u> that she *planned* to leave home.	planned
If anyone has *seen* Vanessa, please contact the	seen
police. <u>Phone</u>: 555-0062.	Phone

1. Missing punctuation is in **bold type**.

2. (i) slim   (ii) white   (iii) olive   (iv) blue

3. Spelling errors are in *italic type*.
   - (a) for, blue, buy, to, seen
   - (b) olive, accent, picture, disappearance, planned

4. (a) Abbreviation answers are <u>underlined</u>.
   weeks, Queensland, years, centimeters, Phone

5. (a) One way of correcting the double negative has been <u>underlined in bold</u>.
   didn't tell anyone that she planned to leave home; told no one that she planned to leave home

Missing Person

Read the description.

Police are concerned (fore, for) the safety of VANESSA
_____

HOYLE. vanessa was last seen two wks ago near her
_____

home in blakeville, Qld.
_____

Vanessa
_____

- is 20 yrs old
_____

- is 172 cm tall and has a slim build
_____

- has ollive skin, short black hair and brown eyes
_____

- speaks with an american acsent
_____

- was wearing (blue, blew) jeans and a white T-shirt
_____

  with a pickture of a cat on it
_____

  at the time of her disapearanse
_____

- may stop at a pharmacy to (by, buy) the medicine
_____

  she needs (too, to) treat her asthma
_____

- didn't tell no one that she planed to leave home.
_____

If anyone has (scene, seen) Vanessa, please contact the
_____

police. Ph: 555-0062.
_____

❶ Punctuation
(a) Find the 3 missing capital letters for proper nouns. Add the missing colon in the offset list and write it in the space at the end of the line.

❷ Grammar
Adjectives describe nouns.

(a) Find adjectives from the text to match these nouns.

   (i)   build   _____

   (ii) T-shirt _____

   (iii) skin   _____

   (iv) jeans   _____

❸ Spelling
(a) Choose the correct spelling from each pair of words in brackets. Write your choice in the space at the end of the line.

(b) Write the correct spelling for the misspelled words in the space at the end of the line.

❹ Vocabulary
Shortened forms of words are often used in text; for example, etc., USA.

(a) There are 5 shortened forms in this text. Write the full version of each word in the space at the end of the line.

❺ Writing
A double negative statement incorrectly uses two negative words.

(a) Underline the line in the text containing a double negative. Write it correctly.

Plant More Trees!

Lesson Focus

Punctuation

- Capital letters for sentence beginnings
- Periods
- Grammatical commas

Grammar

- Verb tense
- Subject-verb agreement

Spelling

- Confused words: by/bye, to/too/two, more/moor, affect/effect
- Misspelled words

Vocabulary

- Enrichment – word definitions

Teacher Information

An exposition can analyze, interpret and evaluate. Its purpose is to persuade by presenting one side of an argument.

Answers

We need to plant *more* trees to prevent the levels of carbon dioxide in the air from rising**,** which would increase the greenhouse *effect* and lead to global *warming***.**

During the *process* of photosynthesis**,** the trees use up carbon dioxide**,** which <u>is</u> a waste product of the human breathing process**.** They then release oxygen**,** which humans <u>need</u> for breathing. **W**e need to plant more trees because their root *systems* hold together fertile *topsoil***.**

When trees are cut down in such great quantities**,** the soil <u>is</u> more vulnerable to erosion *by* wind and water**.** **P**lants are unable to thrive and the land is left *useless***.**

We <u>need</u> to plant more trees to hold the topsoil together so that crops needed for *global* consumption will not be in short supply**.**

We need *to* plant more trees!

more
effect
warming
process
is
need
systems
topsoil
is
by
useless
need
global
to

1. (a) Missing punctuation is in **bold type**.

2. Verbs are <u>underlined</u>.

    (a) is (line 5) need (line 6)

    (b) is (line 9) need (line 12)

3. (a) Spelling errors are in *italic type*.

    more, effect, warming, process, systems, topsoil, by, useless, global, to

4. (a) (i) erosion   (ii) thrive

    (iii) vulnerable   (iv) consumption

Plant More Trees!

Read the exposition.

We need to plant moor trees to prevent the levels of carbon dioxide in _____

the air from rising which would increase the greenhouse affect and _____

lead to global worming _____

during the proccess of photosynthesis the trees use up carbon _____

dioxide which was a waste product of the human breathing process _____

They then release oxygen which humans needed for breathing. _____

we need to plant more trees because their root systerns hold _____

together fertile toppsoil _____

When trees are cut down in such great quantities the soil are more _____

vulnerable to erosion bye wind and water plants are unable to _____

thrive and the land is left useluss. _____

we needs to plant more trees to hold the topsoil together so that _____

crops needed for glowbull consumption will not be in short supply _____

we need too plant more trees! _____

❶ Punctuation
(a) Find the 5 missing capital letters, 5 periods and 5 commas.

❷ Grammar
The tense of a verb must match the time the action occurred. This text is describing a situation that is happening right now, so the verbs are in the present tense.

(a) Find the 2 verbs (lines 5 and 6) which are in the incorrect tense. Write the correction at the end of each line.

Verb endings must agree with the person or people doing the action.

(b) Find the 2 verbs (lines 9 and 12) which disagree with their subject. Write the correction at the end of each line.

❸ Spelling
(a) Highlight the mistakes in the text and write the correction at the end of each line.

❹ Vocabulary
(a) Match these words and definitions.

(vulnerable erosion thrive consumption)

(i) wearing away by wind or water

_____

(ii) to grow well

_____

(iii) open to attack

_____

(iv) using up of goods or services

_____

Treasure Hunt

Lesson Focus

Punctuation

- Capital letters for proper nouns
- Capital letters for sentence beginnings
- Colons in titles
- Colons in offset lists
- Grammatical commas

Grammar

- Indefinite articles: a/an

Spelling

- Misspelled words
- Plurals ("s" and "es")

Writing

- Double negatives

Teacher Information

This procedure outlines how something is done. It gives a list of materials or requirements and instructions using imperative verbs.

Answers

1. Missing punctuation is in **bold type**.

2. (a) (i) an aviary

    (ii) an honest man

    (iii) an old tree

    (iv) a hut

    (v) a useful map

    (vi) an uncle

3. (a) Spelling errors are in *italic type*.

    treasure, energy, Turn, paces, aviary, marked

   (b) These plural nouns are <u>underlined</u>.

    guides, shoes, bushes, crosses

4. (a) One way of correcting the double negative is <u>underlined in bold</u>.

    "Moms and Dads, if you haven't got no energy to take part ..." should read "Moms and Dads, if you **haven't got any** energy to take part ..." or "Moms and Dads, if you **have no** energy to take part ..." or "Moms and Dads if you don't **have any** energy to take part ..."

Bailey Park**:** daily activities

Today's *treasure* hunt starts at 2 p.m**.**
Good luck!

(Moms and Dads, if you haven't got any *energy*/have no *energy* to take part, you can send the kids with one of our volunteer <u>guides</u>.)

You will need**:**

- a shovel

- good walking <u>shoes</u>

What to do**:**

1. Walk to the snack hut and find the rock shaped like a dog.

2. **T**urn toward the swings and walk 20 *paces*.

3. Search under the three <u>bushes</u> directly in front of you. **T**ake one of the number cards hidden underneath**.**

    This is your treasure box number.

4. Walk to the bird *aviary* and ask the keeper to point out the oldest tree in the park**.**

5. Go to the tree**.** Behind it**,** you will see a small sandpit with 10 numbered <u>crosses</u> *marked* on it.

6. **D**ig under the cross with your number to find your treasure box.

Treasure Hunt

Read the procedure.

bailey Park daily activities

Today's tresure hunt starts at 2 p.m
good luck!

(Moms and Dads, if you haven't got no enerjy to take part, you can send the kids with one of our volunteer guide.)

You will need

• a shovel

• good walking shoe

what to do

1. Walk to the snack hut and find the rock shaped like a dog.

2. tern toward the swings and walk 20 pasces.

3. Search under the three bush directly in front of you take one of the number cards hidden underneath this is your treasure box number.

4. Walk to the bird avary and ask the keeper to point out the oldest tree in the park

5. Go to the tree Behind it you will see a small sandpit with 10 numbered cross marcked on it.

6. dig under the cross with your number to find your treasure box.

1 Punctuation

(a) Find the 7 missing capital letters, 4 periods and 1 comma. Add 1 colon in the title and 2 in the offset list.

2 Grammar

When the article "a" is needed before a word beginning with a vowel sound, "an'" is used because it is easier to say; for example, "an egg."

Note:
• Some words beginning with "h" need "an" because the "h" is silent, so the word starts with a vowel sound; for example, an hour.

• Some words beginning with a vowel need "a" because the first sound is not a vowel sound; for example, a utility.

(a) Write "a" or "an" before these words.

(i) _____ aviary   (ii) _____ honest man

(iii) _____ old tree   (iv) _____ hut

(v) _____ useful map (vi) _____ uncle

3 Spelling

(a) Rule a line through each of the 6 misspelled words and write the correction above it.

You can add "s" or "es" to most singular nouns to make them plurals.

(b) There are 4 singular nouns in the text that should be plural. Write them correctly.

_____   _____

_____   _____

4 Writing

A double negative statement incorrectly uses two negative words; for example, "I haven't got no more," should be "I haven't any more" or "I have no more."

(a) Underline the line in the text containing a double negative. Write it correctly.

© World Teachers Press® ~ www.worldteacherspress.com

The Wallace Walking Club

Lesson Focus

Punctuation

- Capital letters for sentence beginnings
- Periods
- Grammatical commas

Grammar

- Verbs: present and past tense
- Conjunctions

Spelling

- Confused words: to/too/two, our/are, meats/meets, of/off, threw/through
- Misspelled words
- Suffix "tion"

Teacher Information

This report, written in the present tense, provides information about an organization.

Answers

The Wallace Walking Club is a recent *addition* to the Wallace Primary School healthy *lifestyle* campaign**.**	addition
	lifestyle
The club promotes walking as an ideal way *to* exercise and enjoy the *benefits* of regular activity**. B**oth staff and students *are* regular participants**.**	to
	benefits
	are
The club *meets* each day after lunch**,** on the school oval**. A** variety of routes**,** each lasting 20 *minutes***,** are enjoyed by the regular *walkers***.**	meets
	minutes
	walkers
The *two* major benefits to members are improved health and the development of new relationships *between* students and staff and students *of* different year groups**.**	two
	between
	of
The popularity of the club has developed *throughout* the term and is expected to continue for *many* more years**.**	throughout
	many

Answers

1. Missing punctuation is in **bold type**.

2. (a) (i) promoted   (ii) met

   (b) Teacher check. Answers may include:

   (i) because, when, as   (ii) When, After

   (iii) as, while, and

3. (a) Spelling errors are in *italic type*.

   addition, lifestyle, to, benefits, are, meets, minutes, walkers, two, between, of, throughout, many

   (b) (i) promotion   (ii) vacation   (iii) nation   (iv) education

   (v) separation   (vi) station

The Wallace Walking Club

Read the report.

the Wallace Walking Club is a recent addishun to the _____

Wallace Primary School healthy lifestile campaign _____

the club promotes walking as a ideal way two exercise _____

and enjoy the benifits of regular activity both staff and _____

students our regular participants _____

the club meats each day after lunch on the school oval _____

a variety of routes each lasting 20 minites are enjoyed by _____

the regular warkers _____

the too major benefits to members are improved health _____

and the development of new relationships betwean _____

students and staff and students off different year groups _____

the popularity of the club has developed threwout the _____

term and is expected to continue for meny more years _____

---

1 Punctuation

(a) The report needs 7 capital letters, 7 periods and 3 commas.

2 Grammar

(a) Find the present tense verbs used to complete these sentences and change them to the past tense.

  (i) The club p_____ walking for exercise.

  (ii) The club m_____ daily.

(b) Use suitable conjunctions to join these sentences.

  (i) I had to walk to school _____ Mom's car wouldn't start.

  (ii) _____ the store opened I bought some milk.

  (iii) The train slowed down _____ I watched it approaching the station.

3 Spelling

(a) Underline the spelling mistake on each line of text and write the correction at the end of the line.

The letters "tion" give the sound "shun" as in the word "communication."

(b) Complete the following words by adding "tion."

  (i) promo_____

  (ii) vaca_____

  (iii) na_____

  (iv) educa_____

  (v) separa_____

  (vi) sta_____

THE WALLACE WALKING CLUB

Improve Your Freestyle Swimming Stroke

Teacher Notes

Lesson Focus

Punctuation

- Capital letters for sentence beginnings
- Periods
- Commas in a list
- Grammatical commas
- Question marks
- Colons in offset lists

Grammar

- Imperative (command) verbs
- Adjectives/Adverbs
- Nouns

Spelling

- Confused words: through/though, strait/straight, through/threw
- Misspelled words

Vocabulary

- Enrichment – word definitions

Teacher Information

This procedure outlines how something is done. It gives a list of requirements and instructions using imperative verbs.

Answers

1. Missing punctuation is in **bold type**.
2. (a) Command verbs are <u>underlined</u>.

   Keep, Use, Accelerate, Bend, Tilt, glance, Take, Extend, return, extend, Exhale, kick, Work

   (b) (i) bent – adj

   (ii) fully – adv.

   (iii) completely – adv.

   (iv) alternately – adv.

   (c) Answers will include:

   elbow, arm, hand, lower arm, head, mouth, face, nose, legs, thighs

3. (a) Spelling errors are in *italic type*.

   through, water, mouth, through, straight

4. (a) (i) accelerate: to increase speed

   (ii) glance: to look quickly

   (iii) extend: to stretch out

   (iv) exhale: to breathe out

Requirements**:**

swimming pool**,** ability to swim freestyle**,** swimming suit**,** goggles**,** swim cap

Method**:**

Keep the elbow bent during the pull phase when the arm is in front of the body**. U**se the hand and lower arm as a paddle**.**

Accelerate the arm movement *through* the push phase until the arm is fully extended behind the body**.**

Bend the elbow to lift the arm and hand clear of the *water***.**

Tilt the head to the side and <u>glance</u> behind at the raised arm**. T**he *mouth* will be just clear of the water**. T**ake a breath**.**

Extend the arm forward and <u>return</u> the face to the water**.**

As the hand enters the water**,** <u>extend</u> it further to catch "still" water before beginning the pull phase**.**

Exhale completely *through* the mouth and nose**.**

At all times**,** <u>kick</u> the legs alternately**. W**ork from the thighs to keep the legs *straight***.**

Evaluation**:**

Has your stroke improved**?**

102   *Editing - Book 3*   © World Teachers Press® ~ www.worldteacherspress.com

Improve Your Freestyle Swimming Stroke

Read the procedure.

Requirements

swimming pool ability to swim freestyle swimming suit goggles swim cap

Method

keep the elbow bent during the pull phase when the arm is in front of the body use the hand and lower arm as a paddle

*accelerate the arm movement (through/ threw) the push phase until the arm is **fully** extended behind the body*

bend the elbow to lift the arm and hand clear of the (warter/water)

*tilt the head to the side and glance behind at the **raised** arm the (mouth/ mowth) will be just clear of the water take a breath*

extend the arm forward and return the face to the water

as the hand enters the water extend it further to catch "still" water before beginning the pull phase

*exhale **completely** (through/though) the mouth and nose*

*at all times kick the legs **alternately** work from the thighs to keep the legs (straight/strait)*

Evaluation:

has your stroke improved

❶ Punctuation
(a) Write in the 13 capital letters, 11 periods, 1 question mark, 2 grammatical commas and 4 in a list. Add 2 colons in offset lists.

❷ Grammar
Command verbs are used to give clear, precise instructions.

(a) Underline the 13 command verbs.

An adverb describes a verb and an adjective describes a noun.

(b) Are these words adjectives (adj.) or adverbs (adv.) in the text? Highlight the correct boxes.

(i)   bent   adv.   adj.

(ii) fully   adv.   adj.

(iii) completely   adv.   adj.

(iv) alternately   adv.   adj.

(c) List 6 nouns referring to body parts.

_____

_____

❸ Spelling
(a) Circle the correct spelling from each pair of words in brackets.

❹ Vocabulary
(a) Find the meaning of the following words.

(i)   accelerate _____

(ii) glance _____

(iii) extend _____

(iv) exhale _____